To Tiziana
From Soel xxx

Christmas
27th December
DUBLIN

AIRBRUSHING AUTOMOBILES

AIRBRUSHING AUTOMOBILES

TIPS, TECHNIQUES AND PROJECTS

NANCY DUIN
PROJECTS ARTIST: VINCENT WAKERLEY

STUDIO
VISTA

STUDIO
VISTA

Copyright © 1989 Quarto Publishing plc

First published in Great Britain in 1989 by
Studio Vista
An imprint of Cassell Publishers Limited
Artillery House, Artillery Row
London SW1P 1RT

British Library Cataloguing in Publication Data
Charlesworth, Andy
   Airbrushing automobiles.
   1. Airbrushing. Manuals
   I. Title
   751.4'94

ISBN 0-289-80005-6

This book was designed and produced by
Quarto Publishing plc
The Old Brewery, 6 Blundell Street
London N7 9BH

Senior Editor: Kate Kirby
Editor: Angie Gair

Picture Research: Jack Buchan
Designer: Graham Davis
Artwork: David Kemp
Photography: Paul Forrester
Model car photography: Colin Barker

Art Director: Moira Clinch
Editorial Director: Carolyn King

Typeset by Ampersand Typesetters, Bournemouth
Manufactured in Hong Kong
by Regent Publishing Services Ltd
Printed by Leefung-Asco Printers Ltd, Hong Kong

Frontispiece: Vincent Wakerley

With special thanks to
Langford & Hill for supplying equipment.

CONTENTS

INTRODUCTION

Although there is a US patent for an airbrush case dating from 1888, the "official" birth of the airbrush was in 1893, when the British watercolour artist Charles Burdick devised a way of applying paint faster and more efficiently than ever before. However, despite the airbrush's obvious ability to grade colour in a much more subtle way than could ever be achieved with a brush, about 70 years were to pass before it became commonly used in the fine arts.

Meanwhile, the airbrush established a niche in the commercial arts. First, it was used in the retouching of photographs – for which it is still employed, either to join together two or more disparate images or simply to remove parts of a picture that are unnecessary to the essential message being conveyed. Its other major use prior to the 1920s was in the decoration of show cards – that most basic of advertisements.

During the 1920s, however, the airbrush really came into its own. In that decade, Henry Ford's automobile assembly line in Detroit was working to capacity: the last of more than 15 million Model Ts was produced in 1927. The automobile was no longer the rich man's toy but an essential mode of transport for everyone – and especially in the United States, where the distances to be covered were vast. Cars became cheaper and more plentiful, and, in addition to Ford in the US, they were produced by such manufacturers as Morris and Austin in the United Kingdom, Citroën in France, Opel in Germany and Fiat in Italy. And after the Great Crash of 1929, cars became cheaper still.

However, the basic equation of cheap cars sold to an enthusiastic mass public demanded one extra ingredient for success: advertising. If enough cars were to be sold to keep costs down, then people had to be made aware of the bargains awaiting them. This was done by featuring advertisements of automobiles in as many places as possible, but particularly in magazines and on posters, both of which were now being printed using the photogravure process. Photogravure eliminated the lines and dots that had made up printed images (and can still be seen in newspaper illustrations today), and resulted instead in pictures formed of smooth ink film. Airbrushing, with its subtle gradations and stipple effects, was a perfect medium for these advertisements.

Following World War I, the march of technology – with its attributes of efficiency and velocity – made a great impact on artists. Machines seemed to create order out of chaos (remember, this was *before* the age of the traffic jam), and artists' awareness of their speed (especially that of automobiles) created, in turn, a new artform: graphic design for advertising. The commercial poster became a major advertising tool, and bold, streamlined images were designed to convey messages in a few brief moments.

By the 1930s, the rough-and-ready automobile advertisements of the previous decade had given way to ones that adopted an air of elegance and sophistication, planting cars squarely on a pristine background and making them look bigger and better than the real thing. In addition, automobiles were promoted to the middle classes as "family cars", comfortable on long journeys and short. However, this safe, cosy picture of society was soon swept aside by the realities of war. The years of World War II were enlivened by a multitude of airbrushed propaganda posters that, perhaps because of the tensions of the time, seemed to reach directly the emotions and fears of the audience at which they were aimed.

Shortly after the war ended, airbrushing experienced a decline in popularity. Why this occurred is still not fully understood, but it may have been because airbrushed images had become associated with the grim times of the Depression and the terrible years of the war. In any event, to the new crop of graphic artists emerging at the end of the 1940s, airbrushing was defi-

The style and stylishness of the 1939 Lincoln-Zephyr V12 has been exaggerated in this advertisement.

The drawing of the car's "skeleton" (below left) is an early example of engineering as a selling feature.

WHERE HAVE THE BAD ROADS GONE?

THOUGH it is not yet recorded on the maps, most roads in America are now first-class. Secondary routes have disappeared. By-paths have leveled off — their ruts and chuck-holes are somehow filled. It's easier now to drive wherever you please!

All this happens when you buy a Lincoln-Zephyr!

A unique combination of features, not to be matched at any price, is responsible for this car's great comfort and safety. First of these is the truss-type construction. Body and frame in closed models are a unit — a rigid, unyielding framework of steel to which steel panels are welded. The whole is then gently cradled on soft transverse springs.

Other features make their distinct contributions to comfort: chair-high seats . . . large interiors (this is a big car) . . . high visibility . . . low center of gravity (steadiness around turns) . . . equal distribution of car weight and passenger weight . . . position of passengers toward the center (where shocks and jolts from the road are less likely to reach).

The V-type Lincoln-built engine is the only "twelve" in the medium-price field. It offers smooth power for all travel. And it is a thrifty "twelve" — under many conditions and many weathers.

You have admired the Lincoln-Zephyr's outward beauty. This *is* the car that set the styles for the industry! Discover now, on roads you once thought closed to travel, the comfort, power, economy and safety *beneath* the Lincoln-Zephyr's style! Lincoln Motor Company, Division of Ford Motor Company.

BENEATH ITS OUTWARD BEAUTY

A combination of features that makes it the only car of its kind. 1. *Unit-body-and-frame—steel panels welded to steel trusses.* 2. *V-type 12-cylinder engine—smooth, quiet, economical power.* 3. *High power-to-weight ratio—low center of gravity.* 4. *Comfort for six, "amidships" in chair-high seats—gliding ride—direct entrance—high visibility.* 5. *Hydraulic brakes.*

Lincoln-Zephyr V·12

THE STYLE LEADER

nitely old hat. The result was its use became restricted to book jackets, comics, music sheets, technical illustration and only a few advertisements. In its place, the paintbrush and, in particular, the camera reigned supreme.

It was not until the 1960s that the airbrush began again to find a sympathetic audience, and the advertisements on which it was now used were different from any that had gone before. The Sixties were an economic boomtime, and with increased money in their pockets, consumers were ripe for all the new designs and goods that were soon available. As well as record sleeves, in which the incredible versatility of the airbrush could be shown to best effect, car advertisements could be given an instant, slick, high-gloss impact that was somehow lacking in photographs.

DREAMS FOR SALE

The work of a partnership of two American artists demonstrated this clearly. Arthur Fitzpatrick and Van Kaufman produced a famous series of advertisements for Pontiac from 1959 to the early 1970s, in which the cars (painted by Fitzpatrick) were set advantageously in sporty surroundings – a dune buggy motor rally, the seaside complete with dinghy – created by Kaufman. In some of their creations, the front of the Pontiac seemed to thrust out of the picture, the rest of the car appeared exaggeratedly long, and the bonnet, shiny and sleek, became the focal point. Through these advertisements, Fitzpatrick and Kaufman were able to bring airbrushing up to date, to allow others to see for the first time the true potential of this technique.

By now, consumers were becoming increasingly interested in the way in which the things they bought actually worked. Gone were the days when car owners simply chose their vehicles on the basis of colour and outward design: now they were far more suspicious of "big business". The automotive industry countered this by an increased use of technical illustration in their consumer advertising – something that had previously been restricted to technical manuals for car workers, repairers and sales personnel. The Ford company in Britain, for example, found that, by doing this, its customers were reassured that the manufacturer was "not trying to get away with anything", even if the average consumer was incapable of truly understanding what these technical illustrations really meant.

The airbrush was an ideal tool for these new consumer advertisements. Armed with expertise in technical drawing, graphic artists could show engines, cutaways of engines and other mechanical components and, with just a light touch of "ghosting", could indicate with the airbrush how good a car would look on the out-

side, too. And, whereas automobiles and other vehicles had previously been portrayed as brand new and unused, they now were shown being operated, their functional character emphasized, with the result that backgrounds became important.

STATUS STYLING

As society became more mobile – and more obsessed with the vehicles that made this possible – cars were becoming art objects in themselves. Classic cars – the Cadillacs and Rolls-Royces that were within the reach of only the very few – were increasingly highly prized, even though (or, perhaps, because) the mounting cost of oil made these petrol-guzzlers ever more anachronistic in a world gripped by an energy crisis. But some were not content to rely on the classics of yesteryear: they had to come up with something completely new, completely unique – the customized car. Soon, strange (and, occasionally, terrible) motorized hybrids were cruising down Van Nys Boulevard in Los Angeles and, later, along London's King's Road, shocking and entertaining passers-by with their exaggerated tailfins, swooping chrome, eye-dazzling colours and ornate decoration (often achieved with an airbrush).

Airbrush artists welcomed all of these as appropriate subjects for their art. Airbrushed pictures of cars soon became acceptable, not only in the advertisements that had always been their habitat, but also as fine art productions – to be hung on a wall and admired. Somehow they came to symbolize, as no other subject could, the direction in which society was travelling in the latter half of the 20th century.

But why take the time and trouble to airbrush a picture of an automobile so that the end product is as lifelike as possible when all you really need to do, if reality is the aim, is to photograph it? There are a number of reasons for opting for the airbrush, ranging from the purely practical to the more esoteric.

As far as advertisers are concerned, airbrushing makes it possible to show a vehicle in the best possible light. A car may appear to be highly realistic, but by simplifying the details, a strong image is produced. This heightened sense of reality is very important: somehow an airbrushed representation seems more real than real, whereas a brush-painted image, no matter how skilfully and elegantly done, gives the impression of being an old-fashioned, pale shadow of the real thing.

The simplicity of this 1939 composition (top right) emphasizes the car's elegance. The rendering of the paintwork has ensured that it is not flashy but a subdued matt.

Although the copy in this American ad of 1939 (right) points out the car's mechanical wonders, the restrained image itself has an almost Japanese feel to it.

CHAPTER 1

APPROACHING THE SUBJECT

REFERENCES

TRANSFERRING AN IMAGE

DRAWING

PLANNING THE IMAGE

THE EFFECTS OF LIGHT

BACKGROUNDS AND MOOD

REFERENCES

It may be possible to draw and airbrush a picture of an automobile simply by using your imagination. However, most airbrush artists who concentrate on this subject compile comprehensive libraries of references on which to base their work.

PRINTED MATERIAL

There are plenty of books and magazines available that contain pictures of cars. Books include general histories of the automobile and the automotive industry, and ones devoted to specific types of cars – from the elegant Rolls-Royce to the sporty Firebird, Camaro and Corvette, and a multitude in between. Racing cars also feature in many volumes, and customized cars have been a more recent popular subject.

Not to be forgotten are the do-it-yourself car maintenance manuals: there is usually at least one available for every common model on the road. With these, there is the added advantage of having photographs showing various engine parts and other components – invaluable if you want to feature any of these. The manuals that come with the cars themselves can also sometimes contain useful drawings and photographs.

There are a huge number of magazines concerned with various aspects of motoring. Motor sports are increasingly popular, and the magazines devoted to them often contain quite detailed and varied views of sometimes spectacular cars. Advertisements in general magazines can also be a source of inspiration, and there are even magazines that concentrate on cars dating from before 1950.

Other sources of printed reference are car manufacturers and dealers. Masses of advertising material and technical information are churned out by manufacturers every year. Much of this is ideal for developing drawings and paintings, but it must be admitted that a great deal of it comprises retouched photographs and airbrushed pictures – perhaps not the best starting point for a composition aiming at realism.

PHOTOGRAPHS

It may be impossible for you to find exactly what you are looking for in books, magazines, brochures or other previously printed material, or you may have a very special automobile in mind – perhaps your own. In these cases, you might consider taking your own photographs,

provided that you have the equipment to do so.

Although a perfectly adequate picture can be created using one photograph, it is far more sensible to take a number of shots from different angles. There are a variety of reasons for this. First, having photographs of more than one aspect of the car will allow you to choose the best, and so you will not have to rely on a single, inadequate, ill-lit shot. In addition, a car body is highly reflective, and the way the light strikes it may cause a particular part to disappear into the glare.

There is another advantage that can be gained by taking photographs. By using monochrome film, the resulting pictures will show the relative values of the colours and highlights (making it easier to change the colour of the car in your picture), and, if you are planning to airbrush in black and white, they will give you a good indication of the correct shades of grey to use.

WHAT TO LOOK FOR

What you want is, ideally, a variety of good, clear photographs of the car you intend to draw and airbrush. These do not have to appear dramatic – with airbrush in hand, you can add all the drama that your imagination demands. What is important is that all aspects of the car as a machine are shown clearly.

Because of reflected light or shadow, or if the car is photographed at a peculiar angle, you may not be able to see and understand how part of the car is constructed, and even if this may only be a minuscule portion of your final artwork, it can be surprisingly obvious if you get it wrong. That is what happened to one of the finest exponents of the airbrush when he created a picture of a sports car (not a subject that was one of his specialities). From the single photograph that he had been given, he carefully recreated all the reflections in the car door. However, through a freak of photography, these reflections gave the impression that the door was dented, and the artist, unaware of how the door was actually constructed, duplicated the "dent" in his picture.

Reflections can also be misleading because you may have no idea what was around the car when it was photographed. This can be especially important when it comes to matching colour. You will also probably not know exactly what the light source was, and in any event, what was appropriate for the photographer may

Car magazines are a prime source of reference for airbrush artists who want to concentrate on automobiles. The range of printed material available is vast, although you may find it difficult to discover more than one photograph of the car you want to recreate.

not be what you have in mind for your picture. Having more than one photograph as reference will help avoid problems, and you should also feel more able to adapt your drawing and airbrushing to your own needs.

In addition, you may discover that it is impossible to obtain a picture of the particular model that you want to airbrush or one that shows it at just the right angle. If this happens to you, you will have to decide whether to give up on the idea altogether or to adapt your drawing, using whatever photographic references you can accumulate. Thus, you might use one photograph showing the car body and others showing various

detailing. You may also have to turn these around in your mind's eye so that, when you draw your car, they are all at the right angle and in the correct perspective.

Having available close-ups of various complicated components can also be a big help. These often appear fuzzy on photographs – indeed, many advertisers employ airbrush artists to retouch such things as wheels and centre caps on photographs to make them clearer.

TRANSFERRING AN IMAGE

Now that you have collected all your references, you will want to begin to construct your picture by making a rough drawing on tracing paper. If you are lucky and are greatly skilled in freehand drawing, you can begin straightaway. If, however, the accuracy needed to produce a good representation of a car is beyond you, there is no need to worry – help is at hand.

There are quite a few ways to transfer images from photographs to paper. If your reference does not need to be saved, you could, theoretically, skip the rough-drawing stage and, after first placing a piece of tracing-down paper in between, simply trace the car on the reference directly on to your artboard. However, as you do this, you may become muddled as to what you have traced and what you haven't, and you will not be able to alter the dimensions of the image of the car. In addition, you really want to make all your mistakes on your rough drawing, not on the artboard, the surface of which can become damaged with too much handling. This drawing can also come in useful later: you can constantly refer to it, and you can even cut masks using the outlines on it.

Perhaps the easiest "indirect" method of trans-ferring an image is simply to photocopy your reference: modern photocopiers can not only reproduce images that are the same size as the originals, but they can also reduce and enlarge them. However, unless areas of light and shadow are very distinct, photocopies of photographs can be very blurry. Still, this will give you an outline to follow which you can trace down on to your support, and you can fill in more details freehand.

THE GRID METHOD

Alternatively, you could try the grid method. For this, you can draw directly on to any reference that does not need to be kept in perfect condition. If the latter is impossible, you can lay tracing paper over the original, or if there are a lot of fiddly details that need to be seen clearly, a piece of clear acetate can be taped over the image. Remember: you don't have to reproduce all of the original; you can simply use part of it – say, just the car – leaving out the background. You could even combine different parts from different automobiles, to make a unique hybrid.

To make a grid, draw a series of lines down the length of the original, and then another series (spaced the same distance apart) across the width, to form a network of squares. The squares can be any size you like – 1.25 cm (½ in) is common – but the scale you choose will very much depend on the intricacy of the original image (the more intricate, the more squares are needed). If only part of the original is full of detail, you could simply subdivide that section into smaller squares.

Once you have done this on the original, you must do the same on your tracing paper. You can reproduce the squares using the same dimensions, or make them larger or smaller, depending on whether you want to enlarge or reduce the image. For example, if your reference is 30 cm (12 in) wide and you want your final picture to be half as big again – that is, 45 cm (18 in) wide – you must increase the dimensions of the squares by 50 per cent, from, say, 1.25 cm (½ in) to 1.9 cm (¾ in). You may find it easier to locate specific squares on both the original and your tracing if you label the horizontal

The grid method is an excellent (and inexpensive) way of transferring an image from one surface to another. Here, a grid drawn on a sheet of acetate has been attached to the photograph. Another grid, on a larger scale, has been drawn on to tracing paper, and the artist is reproducing the images in each square.

lines with a letter and the vertical ones with a number; then each square will have its own identification code.

Now you can transfer your drawing on to the new grid. Taking each square at a time, copy the lines so that they fall within the tracing-paper square in exactly the same way as they do in the original. As long as you have drawn true squares on both the original and the tracing paper, the proportions of the copied drawing should be the same as those of the original. When you have finished drawing all the lines in all the squares, take a close look at your copy; if necessary, smooth out curves or make other alterations.

THE PANTOGRAPH

One step up from the grid method is the pantograph. This somewhat resembles a collapsible yardstick, but, in fact, it comprises four hinged slats of wood or plastic. At one hinge is a pencil lead, and at another is a pointer. As the latter is traced over the original reference, the hinged arms move in such a way that the pencil draws the same image on a separate piece of paper. There are numbered holes along the length of the slats: by moving the pivot points forming the hinges to different holes, you can either enlarge or reduce the copied image.

Pantographs are not that easy to handle, and a little practice is absolutely essential if you are to achieve an accurate final, finished result of which you can be proud.

PROJECTORS

There are a number of different types of projector that can be used to throw an image (in various sizes) on to a surface from which it can be traced. The simplest (and the most likely to be at hand) is a slide projector. You can use either your own slides or you can hire some from a commercial picture library (but if you plan to sell or publish your finished artwork, check whether the library charges extra for this use). Pin a sheet of tracing paper to a wall or screen, turn on the projector, adjust the image to the desired size and trace it.

An overhead projector will transfer an image drawn on to a transparent sheet of acetate; special images can be achieved by combining a number of drawings on several sheets of acetate and projecting these on to the drawing surface. Another technique is to throw an image of a realistic background using a slide projector and another (possibly of a futuristic car) using an overhead projector, to check what the resulting combination will look like.

Finally – and only for the really dedicated amateur and the professional – a Grant projector can reproduce any image (either printed pictures, transparent slides or sheets of acetate) and throw it through tracing paper. It can also enlarge or reduce to almost any degree desired. However, it is a very large piece of equipment, and it is very pricey.

FROM ROUGH DRAWING TO ARTBOARD

Once you have made your rough drawing, you will need to transfer this to your artboard. To do this, place a piece of tracing-down paper between the artboard and the rough drawing, making sure that all three surfaces are securely fastened so that they do not move. Then, using a hard pencil, trace over all the lines on the original; when you remove the tracing paper and the tracing-down paper, you will see a clean copy of your rough drawing on the artboard.

The final step, before you begin airbrushing, is to ensure that the surface of the artboard is absolutely clean. Even if you have gone to a great deal of trouble not to touch the artboard unless your hands are completely spotless, you can still leave fingerprints behind. No ink or paint will stick to these, and you may find that you are left with the perfect image of a thumbprint in the middle of a bright blue sky! To avoid this, "degrease" the artboard prior to airbrushing, using an appropriate cleaning fluid; lighter fluid is very effective.

It may take time to get accustomed to a pantograph, but the result can be very good. The artist holds down one end with his left hand while his right traces round the original reference with the pointer. On the tracing paper, the pencil lead duplicates the same lines. The pantograph has been set to enlarge the image.

DRAWING

Despite its often glamorous image, the automobile is first and foremost a machine. As such, its depiction in any kind of artform demands a firm grasp of technical illustration, especially if you want to break away from simply copying references and create images that are all your own work.

In the past, technical illustration was only used in, for instance, manuals showing spare parts and the maintenance of machinery or, on a sometimes grander scale, for views of the internal workings of machines, produced for manufacturers. Today, however, technical illustration embraces all graphic forms that explain technology – how machines are constructed and how they work – for both the general public and those working in industry and allied fields.

It could be said that, for those who want to try their hands at airbrushing images of automobiles, a logical approach, an eagle eye and methodical preparation are more important than creativity – although creativity does have a special place in the best airbrushed portraits of cars. However, getting the initial drawing right, before any painting is done, is absolutely vital if the end result is

to be something of which you the artist can be proud.

There are special courses available in technical illustration, and if this field interests you, you may get a great deal out of taking one of these. However, by using some of the basic techniques outlined below, and the various drawing aids described, you should, after a little practice, be able to produce acceptable illustrations.

DRAWING TECHNIQUES

Most objects can be broken up and simplified into various component forms: cones, cubes, cylinders. Learning how to draw these correctly – and, ultimately, how to tone and colour them so that they gain solidity and resemble the material from which they are made – is basic to every artist's education.

PERSPECTIVE First, however, it is important to find out about and learn to use perspective. This will enable you to draw objects so that they are in correct relation to each other and appear realistically within space.

Imagine that you are on a flat plain, facing a straight road that vanishes in the distance before you. Although the sides of the road are really as straight as an arrow, as

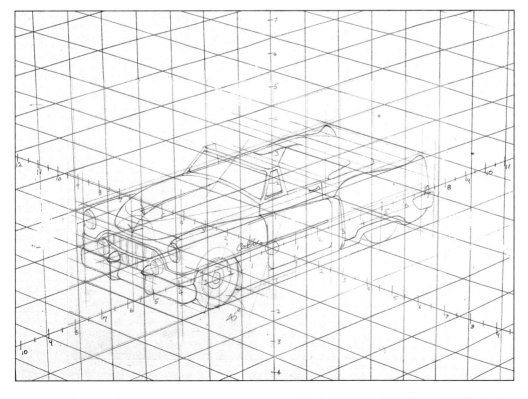

Armed with a perspective grid, artists can forget about drawing lines to vanishing points. The grid itself, a matrix of crossing lines, allows the plotting of coordinates so that perspective can be established. In some, all lines lead to the same vanishing points, but others have lines extending towards a variety of points. Many perspective grids are computer generated.

▲ In the three pictures above left, the photographer has lowered his point of view while the model Cadillac has remained in the same position. In the first picture (top), the car is seen from a relatively normal angle, which might be a good choice if all you are concerned with is rendering as much detail on the automobile as possible. By the time you reach the bottom photograph, however, the vantage point has been lowered almost to ground level. The result is greater distortion and more drama, although detail is lost.

▲ The effect of a changing viewpoint is also examined in this sequence (above right). In the top photograph, the car is seen from quite a way above. This reveals a great deal of the interior as well as the bonnet, but on the whole, it is a rather flat image. In the middle photograph, the vantage point has been lowered, until finally, in the bottom picture, it is about half as high as the top picture. The car has now been given a feeling of movement, with the bonnet thrusting forward and the side elongated.

they recede into the background they appear to converge gradually towards each other until they meet at the horizon – the "vanishing point". This view is known as "single-point perspective" – that is, if the horizontal edges of all the objects in the view could be extended, they would all meet at that one vanishing point. In cases where the actual horizon cannot be seen – inside a room, for instance – it is quite easy to establish the horizon line: simply hold a pencil horizontally in front of your eyes, at arm's length, and compare the angles of edges receding towards it.

If you were to add, say, buildings on either side of the road, you would have to draw the lines forming their tops and bottoms so that they, too, met at the vanishing point (afterwards erasing those portions of the lines that do not appear on the buildings themselves). And if you were to complete the picture by placing a car in front of one of the buildings, the side and top of it that are visible to you would have to be drawn in keeping with the vanishing point. An object can also be drawn above, below or spanning the horizon. If drawn above it, the bottom will be seen; if drawn below, the top will; and if it spans the horizon, neither the top nor the bottom will be seen.

Single-point perspective is, however, only rarely used. Much more common is two-point perspective. In this, there are two vanishing points: one to the left and one to the right. Objects are drawn from an angle – not face on – and the lines forming their tops and bottoms extend (invisibly) back to either the vanishing point on the left or the one on the right. All the lines forming the objects' vertical sides are at right-angles to the horizon.

Many technical illustrations are also produced in three-point perspective, with the object viewed from slightly above. This is similar to two-point perspective in

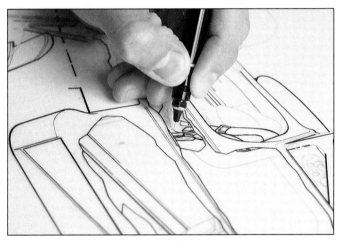

▲ An ink drawing can be sprayed with a transparent medium so that the outlined details stand out. This type of drawing is known as a "keyline". Much of it can be drawn freehand, and there are also a number of drawing tools available.

▼ French curves contain a variety of curves, some more arced than others. A good collection will give you all the types you need. When using a template like this, you have to take care to hold it firmly against the drawing surface.

▲ If your composition is quite technical, a set square can be used to mark right angles. In addition, because of its easy-to-handle size, artists sometimes prefer to use its straight edge rather than a ruler.

▼ Accumulating ellipse guides will ensure that you have the most basic types. A good way to prevent smudging when drawing with ink is to place a guide below the one you are using, with a larger ellipse beneath the one you are drawing.

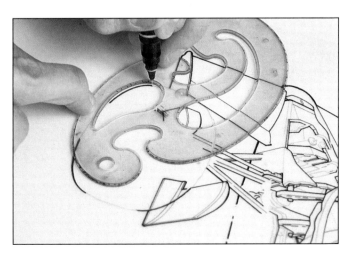

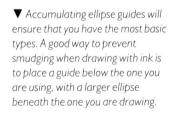

that there are vanishing points to the left and right; however, in addition to these, there is another vanishing point at the bottom of the picture. Therefore, the lines forming the tops of, say, buildings are drawn using the vanishing points on either side, and the lines forming the vertical sides of the buildings extend (invisibly) to the third vanishing point at the bottom.

When first becoming acquainted with perspective, it is helpful to spend some time drawing objects in one-, two- and three-point perspective, extending lines back to the relevant vanishing points and then erasing the parts that are not needed. After such practice, you will probably find that it is quite easy to judge the correct perspective simply by eye, only occasionally using vanishing points and extended lines when a drawing is particularly complicated. In addition, you could also use a perspective grid.

Squares drawn in two- and three-point perspective never have 90-degree angles, and circles all become ellipses. Learning how to handle these different elements correctly will make all the difference when you come to sketch automobiles.

SQUARES AND CIRCLES   Drawing squares so that they are in the proper perspective is quite easy as long as you are careful to construct them using the correct vanishing points. Circles, however, are another matter.

A circle seen from an angle is not perfectly round as one seen face-on would be. Rather, it is an ellipse – a circle that is narrower across one way (the minor axis) and wider across the other (the major axis). Again, you should eventually be able to draw ellipses adequately by eye once you have had a little practice and have honed your observational skills. When drawing or cutting ellipses (or any other form containing arcs) freehand, remember that your hand holding the pencil (or scalpel) will naturally describe a rainbow-shaped arc. To take advantage of the hand's natural ability, first draw one "rainbow", then turn the paper or board around and draw another to complete the ellipse, circle or whatever. Drawing aids can help (*see below*).

However, it is also important to learn how to construct an ellipse more scientifically, so that it is in perspective and has the right proportions. For this, all you need is a strip of paper. This is called a trammel, and any sort can be used as long as it has one straight side.

First, on a sheet of drawing paper or other support, draw one line for the major axis of the ellipse, and then one for its minor axis, making sure that the latter is at right-angles to the major axis. Then, lay the straight side of your paper trammel along the minor axis, so that part of it touches the spot where the major and minor axes meet and it also overlaps one end of the minor axis line.

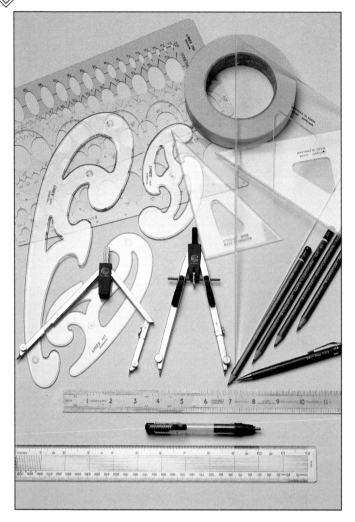

▲ You will have to have the appropriate drawing tools if your creations are to be accurate. Ellipses, French curves and set squares help an unsteady hand; dividers and a compass make parallel lines and circles easy. Two rulers (plastic and metal) are a must, as are pencils, a technical pen and masking tape.

▼ Trying to understand how to use a trammel can be quite hard, but using one is simplicity itself. Here, you can see the piece of paper marked "A", "B" and "C". Marks "B" and "C" remain on their respective axes, and points are plotted at "A". The result in this case is quite an elongated ellipse.

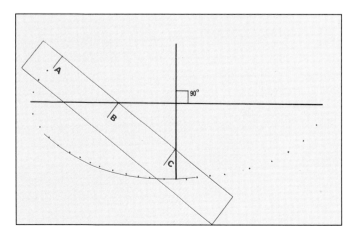

On the trammel, make a mark where the line ends and another one where the two axes meet. Next, lay your trammel along the major axis, so that the mark you made to indicate the end of the minor axis is now at the end of the major axis. Make another mark where the major and minor axes meet. Your trammel now has three marks on it; label the top one "A", the middle one "B" and the bottom one "C".

To construct your ellipse, lay the trammel so that mark "B" touches the major axis and mark "C" touches the minor axis (you can start anywhere). Now make a light dot on your sheet of paper at mark "A". Move the trammel slightly to the left or right, making sure that you keep "B" on the major axis and "C" on the minor axis; make another light dot at "A". Continue plotting a series of dots in all four quadrants until you have described a complete ellipse; then put the trammel to one side, and join up the dots – the more you have plotted, the greater the accuracy when you come to join them up.

Any ellipse can be drawn using this technique, no matter from which angle it is viewed. Just ensure the major and minor axes are at right angles to each other.

DRAWING TOOLS

As we are concerned here with technical illustration as a basis for airbrushing, your drawing implements will usually be pencils: pencil marks are easy to alter, erase completely and cover with paint. If you want to take up technical illustration on its own, or to incorporate some ink line drawing into your airbrush work, you should invest in a good set of technical pens, or one pen and a set of nibs of various widths.

There is a variety of other types of drawing tool, some of which you may already have. These can make technical illustration a great deal easier, and some of them are essential for achieving true accuracy.

RULERS You will continually need to draw straight lines accurately, and to do this, you should have two good rulers. One should be clear plastic and marked in both inches and metric measurements. You will be able to see your drawing through it as you work, which can greatly reduce the possibility of errors. If you plan to use ink, this ruler should have a bevelled straight-edge; the tapering of the bottom away from the drawing surface will help keep smudging to a minimum. (Alternatively, you could simply lay a piece of adhesive tape on the bottom of the ruler, close to but not touching the edge used for drawing.) The other ruler should be steel; this won't be nicked by your scalpel when you cut masks.

SET SQUARES These are the familiar plastic triangles with one right angle. They come in two types, depending on the degrees of the other two angles: either 45° and 45° or 30° and 60°. You will need a set square for, among other things, drawing the axes when constructing ellipses using a trammel. There are also adjustable set squares.

PERSPECTIVE GRIDS These have printed lines radiating from a single point and at various angles. If a grid is placed underneath a piece of tracing paper, any particular viewpoint can be drawn in perspective quickly.

TEMPLATES AND STENCILS Drawing curves, circles and ellipses may seem to be the most difficult of tasks but there are templates to help.

French curves are plastic shapes of various sizes, constructed in such a way that they contain within their swooping edges a number of curves of different radii: you simply choose the portion that matches your needs. Another useful tool is a *flexible curve*, to be used when a curve is particularly complex or uncommon. This consists of a flexible metallic core covered with vinyl, and it will remain in whatever shape it is bent into.

Ellipses guides are also available: these are small sheets of plastic into which have been cut ellipses of various shapes and sizes. A collection of these will provide almost all the ellipses you will encounter, although a good selection can cost a great deal of money. In addition, it is worth noting that these templates should be your tools – you should rule them, not them you. Do not find yourself adapting a drawing to whatever templates you may have: learn how to construct the shape yourself, using the advice given above, and employ this knowledge when you need to.

Lettering stencils can come in handy if you lack confidence in your freehand drawing. However, they cannot be used when you are trying to render, say, a particular car's logo or lettering seen from an angle.

Ideally, all these templates and stencils should have bevelled edges or bosses (small bumps on the underside) to raise them above the drawing surface to prevent smudging; alternatively, you can add strips of tape to just inside the edges, or you can place small rolls of sticky masking tape at the corners. In addition, when drawing ellipses, you can put one plastic guide underneath another so that the ellipse that you want to draw is placed over a larger one below. Templates and stencils (and rulers) can also be used as masks.

COMPASSES These are invaluable for drawing circles and for rendering simple arcs. A springbow compass is adequate for most circles, but if you work on the large scale, a beam compass is essential.

DIVIDERS These are ideal for transferring dimensions from a rough sketch to a final drawing, and for checking that dimensions are correct. They can also be used for marking the same distances a number of times on a drawing – when, say, you have to insert parallel lines.

PLANNING THE IMAGE

Being able to see and understand what you plan to draw (and later airbrush) in all its detail is perhaps the most important element in producing adequate pictures of automobiles. This does not only mean examining the various components of a vehicle – grilles, wing mirrors, tyres, chrome detailing – but also the play of light and shadow on metal and on soft surfaces, the view of the car (foreshortened, its length exaggerated, a difficult angle), the perspective, and which forms (circles, squares, ellipses, cones, cylinders and cubes) make up the different parts.

It is not only the automobile itself that has to be taken into consideration. As we shall see, how the car is lit – from which direction (or directions if there is more than one light source), the intensity and the type of light (natural or artificial) – can dramatically alter how the car appears. In addition, everything else that is included in the composition will not only affect a viewer's impression of the portrait, but because it will all be reflected in the shiny surfaces and will be seen through any transparent glass, it will greatly affect the rendering of the car itself.

By looking closely and carefully at all of the elements of the car that you have chosen to draw, and by carefully considering what you have decided to include in the background, you will be able to isolate the things for which different treatments are necessary – either simply a variation in colour or a completely different airbrush technique. Once you have noted these variations on your initial drawing, you can use this as a guide for cutting masks. You should also begin to plan any brushwork, especially those all-important tiny details that create a strong impression of reality.

If you spend enough time at this early stage just looking and noting, you will save yourself a great deal of trouble later on when you come to airbrush. The result will be a picture of a car that is an accurate facsimile of what you have seen.

▲ This ominous, almost vulture-like view of a Corvette's bonnet by Gavin Macleod basically consists of a limited number of large shapes. The silvery, semi-matt finish demanded great care in the gradating of tones. The grille was rendered by hand, as were many of the details of the car's interior.

▶ In airbrushed portraits, backgrounds and automobiles usually interact, but sometimes it is more dramatic to render a car with hardly any reference to what is behind it. Here, Pete Kelly has combined a pair of relatively two-dimensional images with almost stereoscopic results.

THE EFFECTS OF LIGHT

From the time of the Renaissance, artists have been aware that the way in which a subject is lit can dramatically affect the viewer's response to that subject. The English painter John Constable, for example, described light as "the power which creates space". From the late 19th century, professional photographers have also made increasing use of light and shadow to create atmosphere and send subliminal messages. Airbrush artists producing portraits of automobiles can employ exactly the same techniques, so that illumination and darkness become important elements in their artworks.

If a car is portrayed out of doors, lighting at its most basic will determine the time of day. If the light source is on the horizon, it is either sunrise or sunset, and the shadows will be long and dramatic. If it is high up in the sky, it is near noon, and the shadows will be short, pooling under the automobile. Natural light also gives a very different impression to that of artificial light: it is generally more diffuse, and colours appear more true (ask anyone who has tried to match the correct shade of thread to a piece of material).

Artificial light is more versatile and controllable than the natural light of the sun or moon. Again, the direction of the light source is an important consideration. The same play of shadows can be created as with natural light, but in addition to this, the artist can control the proximity of the light source: if it is relatively far away, the car will remain mainly in the shadows, with only a few areas highlighted; if it is very near, shadows will be fewer and sharper, and the reflective surfaces of the car facing the light will explode with brightness.

You might also try using more than one light source – say, one facing towards the front left-hand side of the car and one towards the front right-hand side. This will eliminate almost all shadows on the front of the car, making what you portray appear flat but clear. However, two or more light sources can play havoc with reflections, and unless you are experienced with handling this and instinctively know how shiny surfaces behave in these circumstances, it is advisable to start by working from photographs that have been lit in this way, rather than trying to imagine what the effect would be.

The warmth or coolness of the light will also make a difference in the ultimate portrayal of the vehicle. Natural light is relatively warm, particularly in late afternoon, but if it bounces off a cool surface such as snow-covered ground, it will take on the blue coldness of that surface. Artificial illumination, on the other hand, can be anything from the coldest, most unforgiving of fluorescent lights to the warm glow of a bonfire. In addition, it can be virtually any colour of the spectrum. All this must be taken on board when the colours of the car's paintwork are rendered: an automobile that you know to be cherry red can, under certain circumstances, take on a peachy tint or can, under others, take on a purplish hue.

The techniques of light and shadow used by the great artists of the past and present can also be incorporated into an airbrushed portrait. For example, in the 19th century, the Impressionists took the art world by storm by using pure, unmixed colours and loose, broken brushstrokes in their paintings to create an illusion of movement and quivering light. Constable, Turner, Caravaggio and, most notably, Rembrandt, were expert practitioners of *chiaroscuro* (from the Italian "light-dark"): while, in general terms, this simply refers to the balance of light and shadow in a picture, it is usually taken to mean pictures in which the subject itself appears to be the source of light, with everything surrounding it in deep shadow – a technique that is inherently dramatic. The influential American artist Edward Hopper, whose streetscapes devoid of people somehow seem to sum up the Depression of the 1930s, created atmosphere by placing his light source directly overhead so that his subject matter appeared flat and piteously stark. And, finally, fashion photographers of the 20th century have become adept at creating illusions of glamour and perfection by covering the lenses of their cameras with gauze, so that the photographed image is almost dream-like with diffuse light and shadow.

Direction, proximity, warmth, colour – all these elements of light can be varied to create an infinite number of effects, and you as the artist must decide how you are going to use them.

Here, a model of a Mercedes has been lit in five different ways – only a few of the almost infinite number of possible variations. **1** The light source is in the front and to the left. Only the front of the car is lit to any great extent, and the result is a relatively flat image. **2** The light source is at the back and to the right. This gives a much more dramatic result, with the sleek lines of the wings and hood highlighted. **4** and **5** The car is lit from, respectively, the right and the left, the result of which greatly emphasizes the car's three dimensions and accentuates various features. **3** The car is lit neutrally from both left and right; while not dramatic, this does give the viewer a clear image of all the car's components.

BACKGROUNDS AND MOOD

Enhancing a portrait of an automobile by rendering a particular mood or atmosphere can be achieved in any number of ways. Lighting, as we have seen, is especially important. In addition, the car itself can take on almost lifelike characteristics. It can be made to look menacing: remember the posters for the film version of Stephen King's *Christine*, the story of a psychopathic car? Or it may appear to be as friendly as a log fire – try airbrushing a scarlet glow just around the edges of a red car.

However, most often a mood is created via the background. Just when this is put in very much depends on the style of the illustrator and on any particular problems arising from the composition – for instance, if a car's transparent glass windows are to be a feature, they must be painted *after* the background has been applied. Whether you put in the background first or last, you must always check that the tones of the background and the central object are not too similar to one another: insufficient tonal contrast results in a flat image that lacks "punch". To avoid this, occasionally lift the corner of the mask to check the background against the subject and alter the tones appropriately.

If you want to make your car the only feature of your painting, you should apply a background of more or less flat colour. However, this does not have to lack depth or texture. You can achieve both in a variety of ways. For example, spray using an airbrush with a blunt needle, or spray the background first at low pressure to get a spatter effect, and then apply a smooth layer of the same colour over the spattering. You could also try spraying at an oblique angle after first underpainting the base colour at the correct angle. If you want to achieve an even more speckled effect, use a mouth diffuser. This is the most basic type of airbrush. The mouth diffuser comprises two hinged tubes, one of which is dipped into the medium and the other blown through to spray the paint unevenly over the surface. A particularly dramatic effect can be achieved by painting directly on to a black surface or by adding a totally black background.

What you add to the background in terms of objects, views, natural phenomena and/or people will greatly alter the look of the final result. Examples could be: a stylized cityscape with or without cheerful neon signs; a seemingly endless prairie with only a line of telephone poles to mark civilization; a snowy landscape

In combination, a background, foreground and car can make a statement that each would not convey individually. With this Lamborghini, sexy girl and sky signalling the dawn of a new day, Vincent Wakerley has created an evocation of a California lifestyle. Technically, the wispy clouds and pastel colours of the sky and the warm skin tones are excellent foils to the hard surface of the car.

with bare tree branches; a blur of racing cars; a forest with rays of sunlight piercing the gloom; an enormous sky filled with the light of the setting sun. Remember that everything you include in your picture will be reflected in the car's metallic bodywork and in its windows. You should keep this in mind as you prepare your drawing.

The inclusion of people, too, can dramatically alter a viewer's response to a picture. In the 1930s, most car advertisements included the cosy image of a mother and father and their two kids just about to take a ride in the country in their new car. A very famous series of American advertisements commissioned by the Fisher carbody manufacturing company in the 1960s and 1970s featured only a car with a beautiful woman draped over it, with the tag line "Body by Fisher". In fact, there is a long tradition of placing pretty, scantily dressed women next to cars. Whether or not this corresponds with your image of women, it does have the advantage of showing the contrast between warm flesh and hard metal to good effect.

▼ *A prosaic background can serve as an effective contrast to a surreal foreground. Here, Robin Koni has created a weird, Daliesque image featuring a melting yellow cab against the skyscrapers of New York.*

▶ *This scene of forest and Porsche was achieved by John Spires using a combination of inks and dyes on photographic paper. The result of streaming sunlight and unusual reflections is highly dramatic.*

CHAPTER 2

BASIC TECHNIQUES

AIRBRUSH EQUIPMENT

MEDIA

HANDLING THE AIRBRUSH

PLANNING YOUR MASKS

HANDLING MASKS

SPRAYING MASKED
IMAGES

OTHER MASKING
TECHNIQUES

AIRBRUSH EQUIPMENT

Most of the techniques used for airbrushing automobiles are the same as those used for airbrushing any other subject. However, there are a few details in this area of specialization that require a little extra attention, and there are also a number of hints and tips that can make creating your own images of cars that much easier.

For this kind of precision airbrushing, only a double-action airbrush will do. The single-action variety simply does not give the degree of control required. The only exception to this rule would be the use of a single-action airbrush or spray gun for covering large areas such as backgrounds. If you can afford it, having two or more airbrushes loaded with different colours available at the same time will greatly reduce the length of time it takes to create a picture. However, be careful not to confuse them: one misplaced blast of black ink on a sun-filled sky can ruin a painting in seconds.

The precision needed for these kinds of pictures also demands a reliable air supply. Cans of compressed air can be temperamental, and the air pressure can vary. A good compressor with an appropriate moisture trap will ensure that you have just the right amount of air at just the right time – every time.

You will also need a number of good-quality sable brushes of varying widths for painting fine details and highlights. A typewriter eraser is very useful for taking out highlights – simply rub out the relevant airbrushed area. A splatter cap is essential, although some airbrush artists prefer flicking paint using a toothbrush.

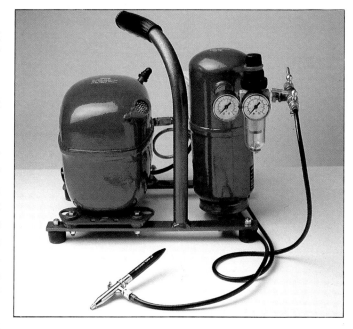

A good compressor will ensure that you get just the right amount of air every time. Make sure that yours *has three important components: moisture trap, pressure regulator and pressure gauge.*

A surgical scalpel with a good supply of sharp blades is an absolute necessity. You will be using this to cut out masks, to scrape away highlights and to get rid of excess paint. You may discover that a round-handled scalpel is easier to use when cutting around curves, and some artists find that curved blades are handier at scraping away highlights.

*For the best results, it is important to cultivate your ability to use a double-action airbrush deftly and efficiently. **1** Hold the airbrush loosely as you would hold a pen, with the middle finger and thumb supporting it underneath, and the forefinger poised to operate the button. **2** Press down the button to release the airflow. **3** While pressing down, pull the button back to release the paint.*

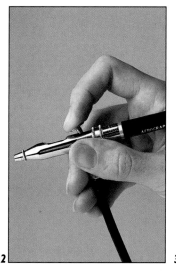

1   2   3

MEDIA

It is, of course, possible to create pictures of auto-mobiles using any sort of media as long as it will go successfully through the airbrush. However, the ones with which you will become most familiar will be watercolour, gouache and, especially, ink.

Watercolour is particularly useful because it is easy to clean out of the airbrush and rarely clogs it. Now-adays, you can buy liquid watercolours in bottles, immediately ready for use. The bottles contain eye-droppers, making it easy to transfer the paint to the colour cup on your airbrush.

Watercolours are transparent, and so can be used to build up tones. This can create a soft, atmospheric effect that, in terms of pictures of automobiles, is probably best employed in backgrounds.

Gouache is opaque watercolour, produced by adding precipitated chalk to a watercolour pigment. Because of its opacity, it hides almost anything that is underneath it – a very useful function if you want to correct mistakes. It is particularly employed to paint highlights on to dark sufaces, even when the rest of the composition has been painted with transparent water-colour or ink. It is best to use permanent white gouache for this – not zinc white, which is for tinting only. It is also not advisable to use gouache too thickly: the surface will become powdery and unstable. The opacity of gouache creates a dull, matt effect.

Ink is a favourite of artists specializing in creating cars, its clean, shiny finish being eminently suitable for reproducing all metallic surfaces such as bodywork

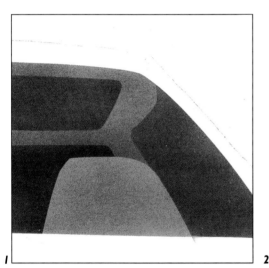

OPAQUE MEDIUM Gouache, because of its covering qualities, can be applied light over dark. Here, the artist has first sprayed a dark tint over the whole interior (1), and then has added the darkest colour – the black of the windscreen wiper (2). Next, he applied the sky reflection on to the glass, using a mixture of white and violet (3), and the remainder of the painting was completed with various tints of red (4). Highlights were added to the roof and windscreen wiper, with airbrush and sable brush.

and chrome. Like watercolour, it comes in handy little bottles with droppers; the latter produce drops of a consistent volume so that, by noting how many drops of each colour you have used, you can duplicate a shade exactly the next time you load your brush. A dozen or so of these little bottles will give you the entire spectrum.

Acrylic paint is also becoming quite popular with airbrush artists. It is diluted and cleaned with water, but it has the drying quality of oil paint.

COLOUR AND TONE

You probably already know quite a bit about mixing colours to achieve various effects. This can be done either by mixing different colours of paint or ink together or by spraying layers of different colours to achieve a completely new final result. However, one aspect of colour and tone that is worth concentrating on if you want to specialize in pictures of automobiles is that of monochromes; in other words, black, white and the full range of greys in between.

Many parts of cars are virtually monochromatic: tyres range from light grey to deepest black; chrome can be rendered in sharp whites and cold, cold greys and light blues. While highlights can be painted straight from a tube of permanent white gouache, and deep shadows can come directly from a bottle of black ink, greys are much more problematical. Some of the best results are achieved by mixing together what may seem to be strange combinations of colours. For example, cobalt blue, raw umber and white can give you a very subtle grey, whereas adding a little sepia to a grey will make the result much warmer.

CHROME

Chrome also creates its own set of problems. It reflects *everything* – even the smallest wheelnut can contain the distorted and miniaturized image of an entire landscape. When producing pictures of automobiles not located in specific surroundings, artists tend to follow custom and practice by ensuring that their chrome reflects brown earth below and blue sky above. And if the chrome-covered part is concave – that is, with a hollow middle – these reflections will be reversed, with the sky on the bottom and the earth on the top.

TRANSPARENT MEDIUM Ink and watercolour, because of their transparency, must be applied in a certain order, either dark to light or light to dark. In this example, the artist began with the darkest element: the windscreen wiper. He then gradually worked through all the tonal values towards the lightest ones. The reflections on the windscreen were the most problematical area: each section of tone had to be dealt with separately, with highlights and background colour intermingling.

HANDLING THE AIRBRUSH

As has been mentioned before, rendering accurate portrayals of automobiles demands a great deal of precision in airbrushing. This is achieved both by the use of a good-quality double-action airbrush and by the amount of practice and care that you devote to your work.

The contours of an automobile are the result of the precision machining of its parts, and if they are reproduced by a hand that is unsure and wavering, the final portrait will be unrealistic and unconvincing. Now is the time to develop a sure touch and an even arm movement by spending some time practising.

First, try some line ruling. You will want to vary the width and sharpness of the lines. Experiment by altering the height of the airbrush from the artboard, and the air and paint/ink flow. As well as doing this freehand, use a variety of straight edges – a ruler (held close to and at a number of different heights from the board), heavy card, a piece of acetate – and see what different effects you can achieve. Since cars also contain rounded shapes as well as straight lines, try out a French curve, ellipse template and other rounded edges.

Control of tones is also vital. A graded tone ("vignette") will give the impression of roundness, whereas contrasting areas of flat tone imply sharp, angular planes. Using strong tones in the foreground and weaker tones in the background creates depth by mimicking the effects of atmospheric perspective. Texture can be modified by altering the proportion of medium to air, or by using a splatter cap.

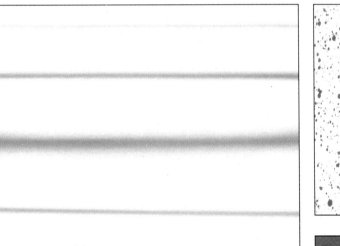

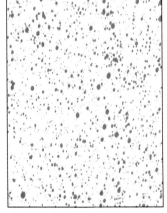

◀ *This splatter effect was created by the removal of the airbrush nozzle and the reduction in the amount of air mixing with the medium. Alternatively, a splatter cap (available for some models of airbrush) will automatically rearrange the air flow, coarsening the distribution of the medium. Cheapest alternative of all is to flick paint or ink on to the surface using a toothbrush!*

▲ *The rendering of these four lines demonstrates the need for correct trigger control and an ability to co-ordinate the distance between the artboard surface and the airbrush. The lines were "drawn" freehand by the artist – that is, no masks were used – but if your hand is not quite as steady, the same effect can be achieved with a ruler, which can either be held in the hand or balanced on an object of the right height.*

▶ *Here a flat colour has been sprayed. Although this appears simple, it actually demands a great deal of control. To eliminate stripes, first spray one way, and then turn the artboard on to its side and spray across the first layer. The graded tone on the right was created by airbrushing in broad, even strokes while gradually increasing the distance of the airbrush from the artboard.*

◀ *Different effects depend on the choice of flat or graded tones and freehand painting or rendering with masks. On the far left, the light yellow circle was created by the freehand spraying of a darker tone outwards from the circle's edge. The dark yellow circle on the left was the result of freehand spraying in a spiral motion from the centre outwards. The harder-edged circles below were achieved with masks: a "positive" mask on the far left, and a "negative" mask on the left.*

▼ *Hard and soft edges and the emphasis of highlights together suggest textures and different surfaces. The upper cylinder was created with a combination of masks and freehand spraying. The one on the bottom needed much more freehand work.*

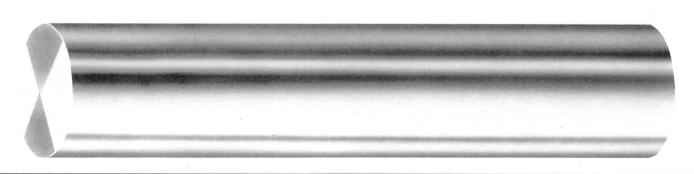

PLANNING YOUR MASKS

If you have created your initial rough drawing carefully, you should be able to judge correctly how many masks you will need. The elements that will demand consideration include: the background, major colours and tones, shadows, reflections, textures and highlights. However, every picture that you attempt to create will have its own specific problems.

However, there is one rule that should be kept in mind: you should try to keep the number of masks to a minimum. This is primarily because you want to avoid cutting into the artboard, which is more likely to happen if you cut a lot of masks.

How you lay your tones – from dark to light or from light to dark – is very much a matter of personal choice. When working in a transparent medium such as water-colour or ink, artists often work from dark to light, since the lightest areas are far more liable to smudging if they are put in first and then further work is carried out on top of them. In addition, the very darkest tones can be sprayed over with other colours and, because the medium is transparent, still not lose their intensity. When working with an opaque medium such as gouache, however, such considerations are not important as most errors and smudges can be corrected simply by being painted over.

Transparent media can also be used to good effect – and fewer masks will be needed – when two colours abut each other. First, one colour is sprayed, and then a mask is removed from an adjoining area and another colour is sprayed over the already-coloured area (creating a new colour) plus the portion of clean artboard that has just been revealed. In effect, this is a method of mixing colours directly on the artboard. It works particularly well when a brown section is next to a red one: first, a yellow-grey mix is sprayed; then, after the next mask is removed, red is sprayed over the whole revealed area. You will find this method especially useful when painting different shades of the same colour on the bodywork of a car, and you should look carefully at your drawing to decide where you might do this.

Transparency will also have to be taken into consideration. An automobile's windows will reveal not only glass but also any objects appearing behind them. These latter will have to be masked and sprayed before a tint is applied to the window areas.

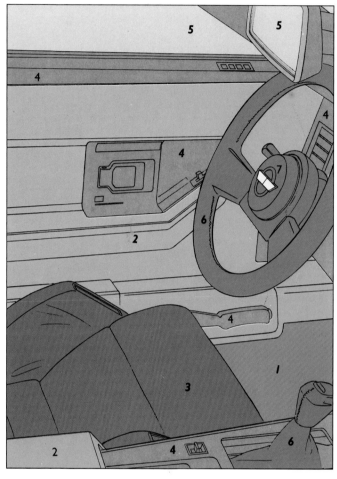

1	Deep-red carpet	5		Window and mirror glass
2	Red panel and console	6		Black/grey leather
3	Red leather seat	7		Steering wheel details
4	Black/grey plastic			

When planning your masking, you must examine carefully all the colours, textures, highlights and reflections you will be dealing with. In this example the artist has had to contend with seven very different types of surface, although only a few colours have been used. Each has been applied in the order in which it has been numbered. Highlights and detailed work have also been carried out, often by hand, as the composition progressed towards completion.

HANDLING MASKS

When contemplating airbrushing, it is easy to forget that all the forms of masking that you will employ are just as important as the airbrush itself. In fact, what type of masking you use and how you use it will determine the finished look of your car portrait.

Low-tack self-adhesive transparent masking film is, today, the most common form of masking employed by airbrush artists, although it wasn't that long ago that they had to make their own by applying rubber-based adhesive to transparent, waterproof paper or tracing paper. Masking film comes in both sheets and rolls, and is thin enough that it can be cut easily with a scalpel. Its adhesive side is protected by a layer of removable backing paper that has to be carefully peeled away as the film is placed over the image. You can also use this paper to hold your masks safely when you remove them to spray, although be aware that the thin plastic film can become distorted and lose its tack so that it may be impossible to reuse masks.

Masking film can be expensive, so if you have to shield large areas from the spray, do this mainly with paper (artists' layout paper is a good choice), using

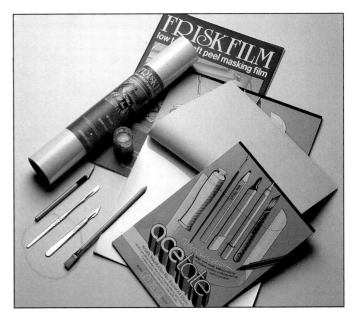

▲ Masking film comes in rolls and sheets; acetate in pads and as single sheets. There are a variety of scalpels, including flat- and round- handled types. A typewriter eraser can be used to rub away highlights, and masking fluid used for masking small details.

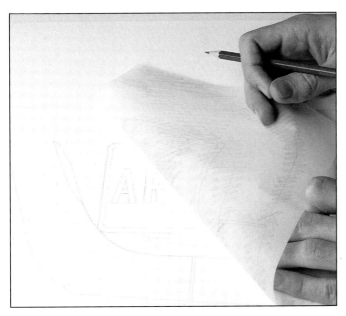

▲ The image has to be transferred from your initial drawing on to the artboard. These lines will determine the number and types of masks – either hard or loose – that will need to be cut. In this particular instance, the number plate will be created with masking film, but loose masks will be used when the bumper is airbrushed.

▲ Masking film should be placed over those parts requiring a hard edge, such as the number plate in this example. First, peel off the paper backing from one corner and attach the film to the artboard. Then stroke the rest of the film over the image, using your hand or the edge of a ruler, peeling off the backing as you go.

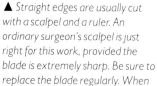

▲ Straight edges are usually cut with a scalpel and a ruler. An ordinary surgeon's scalpel is just right for this work, provided the blade is extremely sharp. Be sure to replace the blade regularly. When cutting masks, be sure to use a steel ruler; a plastic one may have been nicked by a scalpel, resulting in an edge that is not straight.

▲ When curves need to be cut, you can use ellipse templates, French curves and other devices designed for this purpose, or if the curve is complicated (as on this wing mirror), you can do this freehand. Some airbrush artists find that employing a round-handled scalpel makes it much easier to achieve accurate curves.

masking film only over the area on which you will be cutting masks and painting. This technique also avoids the problem of pulling up paint with the masking film, which might arise if you rest your arm or hand on the film while working on another part of the picture.

Learning to cut masking film without marring the artboard underneath will take some time. The pressure you apply to the scalpel should be just enought to cut the film, and a smooth movement will help in achieving this. A cut artboard will result in ragged lines in your artwork, and it is usually not possible to cover these up.

Masking film will give you what is known as a "hard mask" look: in other words, the final image will have a clear, crisp outline. This is because the film is physically attached to the surface, so no paint or ink can creep under the edges, and it is also extremely thin, preventing an excessive build-up of paint at the edges. For something softer, you can cut out "loose masks" from acetate, which, because this material is so durable, can be used again and again. Since these masks do not adhere firmly to the surface of the artboard, some of the spray will get under the edges, creating diffused images.

▲ To remove masking film, either because you have completed that section or to remove a mask, place your scalpel so that the blade is flat on the surface of the artboard. Very lightly pick at the edge of the film until it comes away from the board, and then carefully peel off the remainder of the film.

SPRAYING MASKED IMAGES

With both hard and loose masks, you should generally be careful to spray at right-angles to the surface. Otherwise, there may be a build-up of paint or ink at the edges of the mask (if it touches the artboard surface), or a thin white line might remain where the spray has passed right over the edge of the mask, leaving a sliver of the artboard untouched. This is not such a problem with masking film because it is so thin, but if you place a relatively thick loose mask directly on to the artboard, you may run into trouble. Despite this warning, you should not feel inhibited about experimenting with the angle of spray.

As we have seen, masking film will automatically give a hard edge to any image masked by it. In addition, the effect created by spraying a hard mask can vary from an equally hard, flat colour to a softly gradated vignette (see *Handling the Airbrush* for other ideas).

However, much more variety can be achieved with loose masks. By varying the distance between, say, a loose acetate mask and the artboard, you can vary both the tone and the sharpness of the image. If you hold the mask close to the surface, less of the spray will escape underneath it and thus the image will be more distinct. This ability to alter tone simply by moving a loose mask closer to or further away from the board's surface enables you to achieve a number of effects without having to cut too many masks. You will find this particularly useful when spraying shadows, and by moving a mask in the direction that a car is supposed to be travelling, you can create a blurred effect that gives the illusion of movement.

In addition to acetate, another common loose mask is torn paper. The effects that can be achieved with this will vary, depending on the hardness of the paper used – tracing paper will give a crisp edge and blotting paper will give a soft one – and on the distances between it, the artboard and the airbrush. One trick employed by airbrush artists specializing in cars is to tear a piece of paper, position the two pieces slightly apart and spray the space in between: this results in a highly realistic representation of the reflection in, say, a wing or other metallic surface.

Since spraying will eventually obscure the image, and some of it may already be covered by layout paper, you must take care not to become confused about the varying tones in your image. If you cannot see the

▲ *Masks cut out of masking film will have the clean edges so necessary to the portrayal of a car's precision-made components. By gradating tones, you can make these objects look three dimensional.*

▼ *Loose acetate masks are excellent for creating shadows, especially as these will often become less distinct the further they are from the light source or from the viewer's eye.*

totality of the picture as you go along, you may find yourself creating a background of the same intensity as the car you are portraying, resulting in a picture that lacks definition and, like a bad photograph, appears either under- or over-exposed. The same thing can happen with different parts of an artwork. To avoid this, make a point of lifting the masking regularly to check the balance of tone and colour.

OTHER MASKING TECHNIQUES

So far, we have discussed masking film and loose masks made of acetate and torn paper. However, the number of other things that can be used as masks is restricted only by your imagination.

Plastic templates, French curves and rulers – so important in your initial drawing – can also be used at this later stage as masks. They have the added advantage that they can be simply washed or wiped clean and reused, either on another picture or in a repeated sequence in the same one.

Spraying "found objects" – twigs, leaves, pine cones, fabrics, drawing pins, cotton wool – can result in unique effects.

Despite its drawbacks, masking fluid can be effectively used in a number of ways. As well as its traditional role as a mask for small, fiddly areas, it can be more liberally employed to create texture – for example, by splattering it on to the surface with a toothbrush.

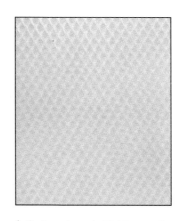

▲ *Ordinary household objects and materials can be employed as masks to create an infinite number of effects. Here, a colour has been sprayed through gauze: the material on the left is more tightly woven than the one on the right. Other* *fabrics that can be used are embroidery canvas, cotton scrim and rug canvas – but the choice is endless.*

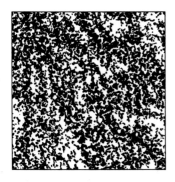
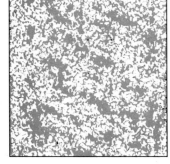

▲ *"Instant texture" can be used as a mask. Above, it is rubbed down on to the artboard. Then, above right, a colour is sprayed over it. This is allowed to dry and then the texture is removed with masking tape. A negative image of the texture is the result.*

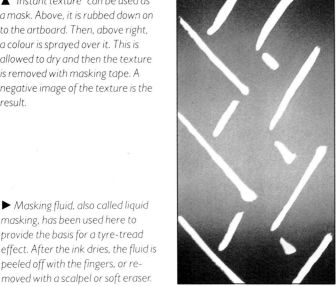

▶ *Masking fluid, also called liquid masking, has been used here to provide the basis for a tyre-tread effect. After the ink dries, the fluid is peeled off with the fingers, or removed with a scalpel or soft eraser.*

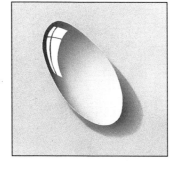

▲ *Rendering a droplet. First, the droplet was masked and the background sprayed. Then the gradated shadow of the droplet was added. The first mask was removed and a "negative" one was cut, incorporating the window reflection. The droplet was then sprayed. Finally, all* *masking was removed and a light blue tint was sprayed over the whole surface. Subtle highlights were added to the droplet and shadow by rubbing with an ink eraser.*

PROJECTS AND EXAMPLES

PAINTWORK

When rendering the paintwork of automobiles, you not only have to deal with the colour of the paint but also with the metallic surface that it creates. In addition, some indication – however subtle – should be given that, beneath the glossy exterior, there is a piece of heavy machinery, something that is solid and substantial. However, what will occupy most of your time and your talent will be the interplay of colour, shadows and reflections. The car that you will be creating must appear the appropriate shade, and this must be toned in such a way that the vehicle appears to be truly three-dimensional. Complicating this fairly straightforward operation are the reflections, which must incorporate the surroundings as well as the contours of the automobile itself. Great care is needed at the initial drawing stage to get all these elements right.

1 *The image of the front right-hand side of this Camaro is first carefully drawn on tracing paper – including all the reflections. Then it is transferred on to the artboard using tracing-down paper.*

2 *The parts of the artboard not to be painted are covered with paper to protect them. Low-tack masking film is placed over the drawing. The film is cut to reveal all the darkest areas: tyre (showing a hint of tread), shadow under the car, grille, around the lights, interior.*

3 *The tyre tread, the very darkest area, is sprayed with black ink. The mask is then removed from the tyre and the tyre itself is sprayed, slightly lighter in tone than the tread and lighter still towards the top and edge. Shadow beneath the car and grille are also sprayed.*

4 *Next the headlamp and sidelight are tackled. Their surrounds are sprayed, the tone of the black gradually decreasing from quite dark at the top to less so on the lower half, to indicate that natural light is just able to make its presence felt there.*

5 *The dark parts of the windscreen and interior are dealt with next. The shadow of the windscreen surround is sprayed first. Then, with a darker spray, the surround itself and the visible parts of the interior are completed.*

6 *The remaining masking film is removed from the interior, and a blue tint is sprayed over the whole area: this begins to give the impression of glass in the windscreen. Then all the masks are taken off to reveal what has been done so far.*

7 *The image is covered again with a new sheet of low-tack masking film. This time, masks are cut for all parts of the bodywork. Great care is taken so that the new masks take account of all the reflections, which are cut as accurately as possible.*

8 The spraying of the red paint-work is begun. The darkest areas are completed first. Acetate masks are used for the softer reflections, the spray just entering the underside of the masks, which are not fastened down.

9 Because the light source is above the car, the reflections under the front are in shadow; thus, they have to be sprayed a darker shade than those around the lights and on the bonnet. Careful use of the airbrush is needed to achieve this distinction. The painting of the wing mirror is also begun.

10 The artist gradually works towards the lighter colours, removing each mask in turn. All the reflections are built up, particularly those created by the windscreen and the bulges of the headlamps.

11 The remaining masks are removed, and the lightest red of all is sprayed on to the appropriate parts. Freehand airbrushing and loose acetate masks are used to soften some of the edges. A space on the front of the car where the number plate will be inserted is left blank.

12 A very fine tint of colour is sprayed over the whole car body to cover any remaining areas of white artboard. Most reflections on a car – that is, all except for a very few highlights – will not be pure white, but will be tinted to a greater or lesser extent.

13 Now the more obvious highlights are added. White gouache is sprayed through loose acetate masks over the red ink. A certain amount of modelling is necessary to give the car the appearance of a three-dimensional object. Then all the remaining masks are removed.

14 The artist completes the paintwork by applying finer highlights, using white gouache and a brush as well as gently scratching back with a scalpel. By comparing this picture with the previous one, you will see that the paintwork now has a much crisper appearance.

MORE PROFESSIONAL EXAMPLES

▲ The chief feature of this Lamborghini created by Pete Kelly is the play of light over the black paintwork. At first glance, the car seems to stand in isolation. However, a closer look at the reflections on the right side will reveal a range of mountains.

▶ The paintwork of this Spanish Fiat Ronda was airbrushed in rainbow colours by John Harwood to show that the car was available in any shade. Inks and acrylics were used, and the colours were carefully graduated so that they blended into one another.

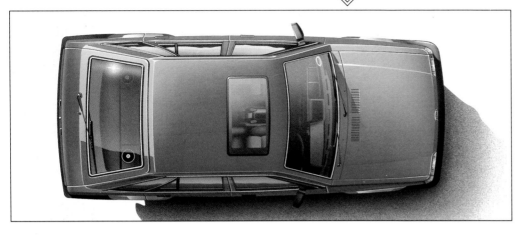

◀ This top view of a Ford Escort by John Harwood was only one of a series that, together, implied a moving vehicle. The shading of the paintwork was gently graduated, with the light source to the left of the car. The rectangular highlighted area on the back was added for interest.

▶ The sleek lines of this Volkswagen Jetta C have been accentuated by artist John Harwood by his judicious use of highlighting on the paintwork below the side windows. This automobile portrait is an excellent example of how simplifying an image can create a greater impact.

▼ Approximately 85 per cent of the paintwork of this Suzuki SJ413JX was rendered using hard masking. The remainder was created with loose acetate and torn paper masks. A limited number of colours – black, white and blue – was necessary because this portrait was to be reproduced in newspapers.

This portrait of a Porsche 959 was needed in a hurry, and Vincent Wakerley was forced to keep all the reflections simple. The result is surprisingly effective, with the shining silver of the car body given a sleekness by the simplicity of line.

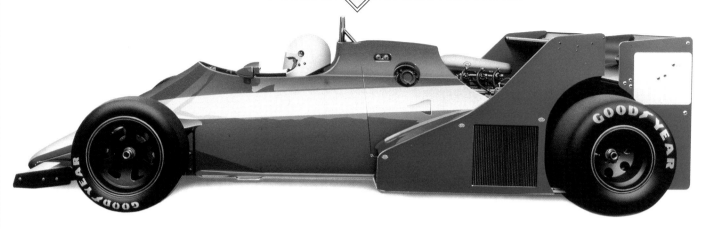

▲ *The paintwork of this Honda Formula One racing car by John Harwood is completely plain because the portrait was used as an illustration for potential sponsors. The oil cooler on the side was created with pen work and scratching back the ink.*

◄ *The rendering of this Keith Harmer portrait of the Jaguar XJR-9, winner at Daytona in January 1988, was complicated by the multiplicity of elements in the paintwork – shadows, reflections and logos – all demanding special treatment.*

► *The style of this splendid Lamborghini portrait by Pete Kelly was deliberately kept simple – for example, flat yellow paintwork rather than high-gloss reflections. The mountains in the background were achieved using torn wrapping paper as a mask.*

◄ *Despite the high technology involved in the vehicle's construction, this portrait of a BMW racing car by John Harwood has an almost old-fashioned feel about it, due to the colours – antique yellow and sepia – of its paintwork.*

Although the tyres are missing from this West German Ford Sierra, this portrait by John Harwood was created to advertise tyres! To create the spray, liquid masking was applied and, when dry, painted over; it was then rubbed off. The water drops on the bonnet were rendered with a brush.

◄ When creating this ink portrait of a 1940s Buick, Pete Kelly was determined to give it a misty "feel" He did this by limiting the amount of paint sprayed and letting some of the artboard show through. The only exception to this was the motel sign, giving it a distinctive neon effect.

◄ Exaggerated rendering of reflection on the side of this car, created by Robert Corley, results in a believable three-dimensional vehicle. Much hard masking was used, with only a light touch of modelling here and there and some subtle tints oversprayed. The lines at the bottom echo the horizon.

▼ Drama is the keynote in Gavin Macleod's Ferrari portrait. The black reflection of hills in the side of the car virtually melts into the deep shadow beneath, the velvety darkness broken only by subtly rendered highlights.

LIGHTS

Airbrushing headlamps and sidelights accurately involves confronting a number of problems. For one thing, they are shiny and will reflect their surroundings. For another, their lenses are made of thick moulded glass, the treatment of which is quite different from that of the simple transparency of a windscreen. They contain concave reflectors, which will reverse and distort all the reflections in them. These particular lights present additional problems: the sidelight is covered with yellow (not clear) glass and is much more recessed into the bodywork than the headlamp. Although they will receive similar treatment, these and other differences must be kept constantly in mind. In this picture, the lights face the viewer directly, and because of this, it is important to get them just right – not to do so will ruin the entire composition.

1 *The entire illustration is covered with paper, except for the two lights. The drawing of the lights is then traced on to the artboard. This contains all the details of the moulded glass and some indication of the reflections.*

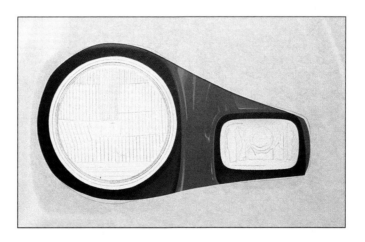

2 *The area not hidden by the paper is then covered in low-tack masking film. Two masks of the headlamp's outer rim (the rim and its shadow) are then carefully cut. This is a precision job, and you might want to try using a scalpel with a swivel blade.*

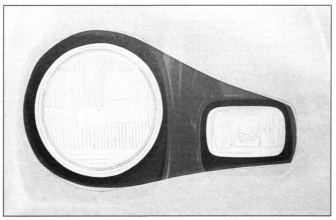

3 *The circular mask covering the darkest part of the rim – that is, the shadow – is removed. This area is then sprayed with a dark blue-grey ink, which will give the shadow of the rim (which is made of chrome) a metallic feel.*

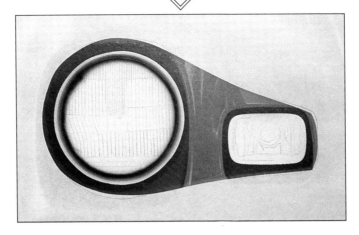

4 *Next, the mask covering the outer – and lighter – part of the rim is removed. This, and the previously painted part of the rim, are sprayed with light grey ink. The artist graduates the colour of this area to a blue reflection.*

5 *Using white gouache and a fine sable brush, the artist meticulously adds some highlights to the rim, to give an even greater impression of roundness. This could also be accomplished by carefully scratching back the black and grey ink with a scalpel.*

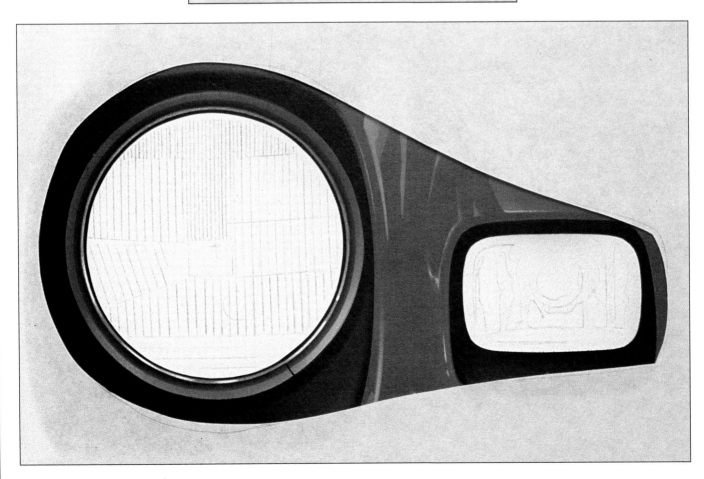

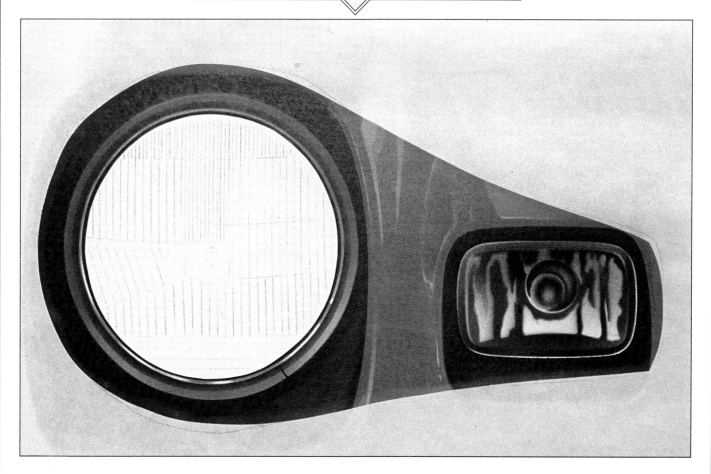

6 *The used masking film is removed, and the illustration is re-covered with new film. The lens areas of both lights are then cut out. Using loose acetate masks and black ink, the artist begins to build up the distorted reflections in the concave reflector of the sidelight.*

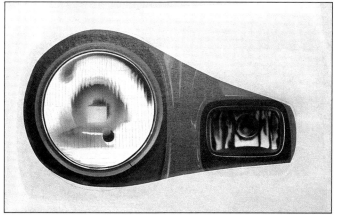

7 *The reflections within the reflector of the headlamp are also dealt with, although there is much less detail needed here than in the sidelight. The artist works carefully and gradually from the dark reflections and shadows to those that are lighter.*

8 *Reflections of blue sky are needed in both lights. Because the reflectors are concave, the sky appears in the bottom of the two dishes: if they had been flat or convex, the reflections would have been on the top.*

9 *More work is needed on the sidelight. Some very precise reflections are inserted using white gouache and a brush (a scalpel could also be used) to indicate its ribbed reflector and smooth lens. Then a tint of yellow is sprayed over the entire sidelight.*

10 *Now it is the turn of the headlamp, which has a smooth reflector and ribbed lens. Using a brush (again, a scalpel could also be employed), the artist adds highlights, carefully following the ribbed pattern as shown on the original drawing.*

11 *White gouache highlights are sprayed freehand on to the headlamp. A very light reflection is added to the recessed sidelight with the aid of a loose acetate mask. The small silver screws in the surrounds are painted with thin grey gouache and a fine brush.*

WINDSCREEN

Rendering a windscreen may not involve as many steps as airbrushing headlamps and sidelights, but here there is a different problem. Clear, highly polished glass reflects its surroundings almost like a mirror – yet reproducing every reflection and highlight can actually ruin the impression of transparency. Here, in effect, less is more. Getting the contour of the window right is of the utmost importance, and this is done by the careful distortion of whatever is reflected in it. What that may be is up to you as the artist. In the illustration here, only a few wisps of cloud are seen; this lack of detail means that the windscreen does not interfere with the overall impact of the whole car. However, you could create a mysterious or surreal impression by having your car stand in isolation, yet cause its windscreen to reflect a scene of great detail.

1 *The illustration is again covered with paper, and this time the windscreen area is revealed. Low-tack masking film is placed over this, and a mask of the glass area is cut out and removed.*

2 *Using loose acetate masks, the artist sprays white, distorted clouds, streaking down the curve of the glass. The clouds are thin and feathery, not a solid mass, and a number of "streaks", ranging from light grey to white, are necessary to indicate this.*

NUMBER PLATE

Number plates are a strategically important part of every portrait of an automobile. Not only are they necessary simply because every car on the road has one, they also give an aura of reality to an illustration as well as providing tantalizing information about a car. The shape and size of a number plate will tell you something about where the car "lives": here, the plate takes the form found in the United States – just right for that all-American vehicle, the Camaro. However, what appears on this plate is not what is found on the highways and byways of the US of A: it is obviously a specialized plate for a very special car. When you render number plates, you will need to employ many of the skills of technical drawing and pay close attention to detail if you are to achieve the precision of machine-made lettering.

1 The area around the plate is covered with paper and the drawing is traced down. Low-tack masking film is placed over this. The larger letters and numbers and the border are cut out and then, using ink, sprayed a solid black.

2 The masking film is removed, and the smaller letters and numbers are painted by hand with a fine sable brush. Great control is needed to do this. If mistakes are made, they can be rectified by carefully scraping back the ink with a scalpel, or by painting over them with white gouache.

3 The letters and numbers are slightly raised so there has to be a subtle shadow below and to the right of each one. The plate is covered with masking film, and a mask of the larger letters and numbers is cut so that it extends slightly to the right of and below each element.

4 Using a light grey ink, the artist sprays over the mask to create the shadows cast by the larger letters and numbers. (The shadows of the smaller letters and numbers will be painted by hand at a later stage.)

5 The masking film is removed from the plate, and then the whole area is sprayed a very light grey. With the aid of a loose acetate mask (torn paper would do equally well), a subtle, slightly darker grey reflection is added to the lower portion of the plate.

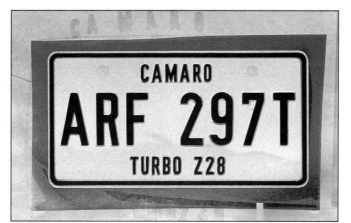

6 Using light grey gouache and a fine sable brush, the artist paints the shadows cast by the smaller lettering and numbers. The amount of shadow cast should be of the same proportions as those of the larger elements.

7 Masking film is again applied, this time to cover the screw heads. A mask is cut incorporating all the details of the screws. Then the film over the slots in the screws is removed, ready for spraying.

8 The slots are sprayed a dark grey. Then the outer, circular edges of the masks are removed and placed on one side. Graduated grey shadows are sprayed, darkest on the lower right side and gradually becoming lighter as they come up the sides of the screw heads.

9 The masks of the outer edges are put back on over the screw heads, and the masks of the centre halves are then removed. These are sprayed a very light, flat grey, to give the impression that they consist of unpainted metal.

10 The screw heads are now finished, and all the masks are removed to check the final result. Any overspraying or excess paint is removed with a scalpel so that the appearance of the screw heads is as mechanically "perfect" as the rest of the car.

FINAL DETAILS

Attention to detail is vital when creating a portrait of an automobile. Not only will car buffs delight in criticizing your work if you should happen to get one small element wrong, but even the uninitiated will develop the impression that something is awry if just the tiniest amount of error has crept in. Cars are so much a part of our everyday lives that we develop a familiarity with every component of them, even if we are not aware that we are doing so. Therefore, the work lavished on the most insignificant bracket, screw or fastener will not be wasted effort. As you near the completion of your picture, now is the time to bring your observational skills to the fore – to spot any shadows or highlights that may be missing, to rectify any contours that may not be true, to look for that glaring mistake that you have somehow failed to see.

1 *Low-tack masking film is placed over the windscreen surround, clamps, hood fasteners and tow bracket. The film over these elements is then cut out and removed, and the components are sprayed with the colour.*

2 *Using loose acetate masks, the artist sprays highlights of white gouache on to the windscreen surround and the clamps. Suddenly, these components take on a three-dimensional form.*

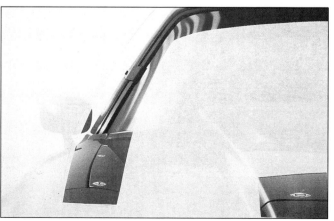

3 *Shadows and highlights are added to the hood fasteners by hand, with a fine brush. Then all the masking film is removed and the picture is checked. At this final stage, a few highlights are added freehand with the airbrush.*

CAMARO
ARF 297T
TURBO Z28

MORE PROFESSIONAL EXAMPLES

▶ When faced with creating variation in the large white bonnet of this E-type Jaguar, Pete Kelly chose to render the glass of the headlamp in a yellow tint, and ensured that the orange of the right indicator was echoed in the sand dunes beyond.

▶ This London taxi by Gavin Macleod is in the midst of Piccadilly Circus. With such an active background, the artist decided not to make the windscreen reflection realistic but to keep it simple and abstract. Some of the dark streaks were hard-masked; others were created with a soft paper mask.

▼ The subject of this painting, created by Keith Harmer, is a customized Ferrari. To give greater impact, the windows have been simplified. In real life, what was behind them would have shown through to some extent, but the artist decided to render just an abstract reflection.

◀ In a Berlinetta Ferrari, the back lifts up and so the back window cannot slope. Pete Kelly indicated this by painting a highlight on the window that gives the illusion of the window angling forward. The tail lights were simplified to give increased impact to the picture.

▼ Interest can be added to a car portrait by including an unexpected reflection in a window. For this Testarossa Ferrari, Pete Kelly added the reflection of a tree in the windscreen. First, this was sprayed black (with a little red showing through); then white gouache was used for the sky.

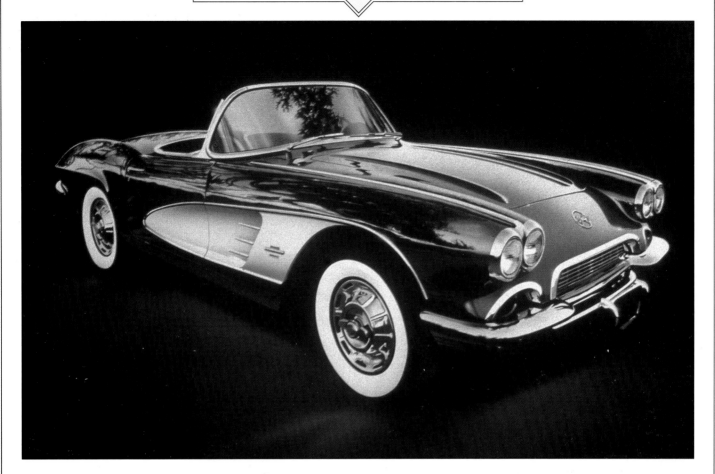

▲ This Pete Kelly portrait of a Corvette is an excellent example of the use of ink for paintwork. The crisp impact is felt even in the windscreen, where, again, trees are reflected. These were hand painted as a negative – that is, white gouache outlines formed the leaves and branches.

▶ The bulbous headlamps of this Mercedes 300SL "Gullwing" are centre stage, and were created by Pete Kelly, using a sable brush. First, a thin wash of blue was applied, which was built up to take in reflections and shadows. Then white highlights were added in gouache.

A surreal impression has been created by John Harwood with reflections of two very different mountain ranges in the bonnet and windscreen of this Ford Scorpio. The mountains were achieved by the use of acetate masks combined with torn paper. To render the dust raised by the car, opaque white was sprayed freehand and then colour applied on top.

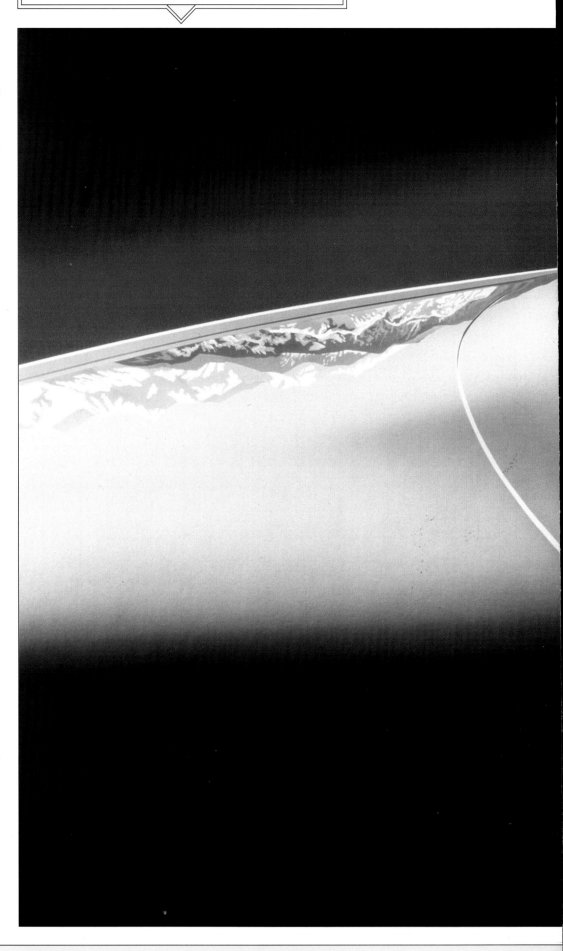

◀ *The reflection in the windscreen of this Porsche 930 Turbo coupé by Gavin Macleod was achieved by hard masking and spraying a tint of grey ink over the already sprayed blue-to-white glass. The white detail on the headlamp was done with a brush, the artist holding a ruler as a guide.*

▶ *The exuberant detailing of this Chevrolet Impala was rendered immaculately by John Spires in ink and gouache. The concavity of the headlamp reflectors has resulted in a completely reversed image of the reflected landscape.*

INTERIORS

The interiors of automobiles present airbrush artists with a multiplicity of challenges. Not only are there a variety of shapes – ranging from the smooth ellipse of the steering wheel to the sometimes quite complex arrangements of recessed door handles – but the textures can vary quite dramatically: the wool carpet of the footwell, the matt plastic of the dashboard and mirror surround, the shiny plastic of the indicator, the cloth, plastic or leather of the seats. Heavy, textured leather that is stitched together is also a frequent feature; it is seen on the steering wheel and gear shift in the following sequence. Although this could be laboriously reproduced by hand, a much quicker solution is to use as a mask "instant texture", similar in composition to instant lettering and made by most of the same manufacturers.

1 *The interior to be airbrushed is drawn carefully on to tracing paper. Only the broad outlines of the leather seat are included at this stage: the details of the creases and highlights will be rendered freehand at a later stage.*

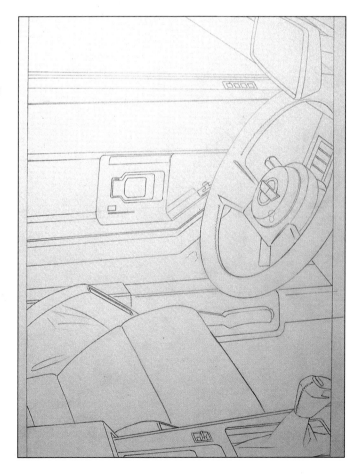

2 *The drawing is traced down on to the artboard, which the artist has scrupulously cleaned. Paper is secured over the entire surface except in the area of the footwell carpet. This is covered with masking film, and a mask of the footwell carpet is cut and removed.*

3 *A deep shade of red ink is mixed in a small dish. The artist dips a paper kitchen towel into this and then lightly dabs the ink-soaked paper over the revealed artboard until the texture is even throughout. This is an excellent method for achieving the nubbly texture of carpet.*

4 *A tint of red is then sprayed over this area of texture, to give it form and continuity. A darker shade is sprayed for the shadows. The result of these various treatments and layers of colour is a distinct texture, quite different from those of other parts.*

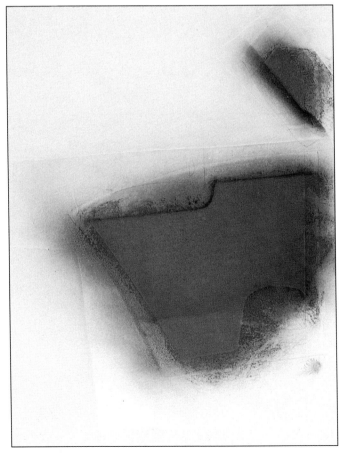

5 *All the used masking is removed and replaced with clean paper and masking film. This time, the area of concentration is the door panel, including the arm rest but not the door handle and light; the red central console armrest is also dealt with. Masks are cut for the relevant parts.*

6 *Working from dark to light, the artist first sprays in the shadows. He uses both loose acetate masks and a ruler to achieve the soft edges needed. The line along the inner edge of the armrest requires the greatest care.*

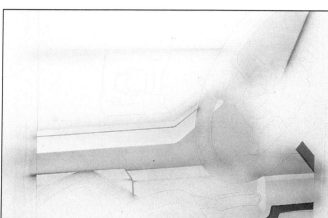

7 *The masks covering the lighter areas of the panels are then removed. Red ink is sprayed over everything, including the already-sprayed shadows. Through this layering of tint on tint, the correct balance of tones is achieved, giving a realistic illusion of shape.*

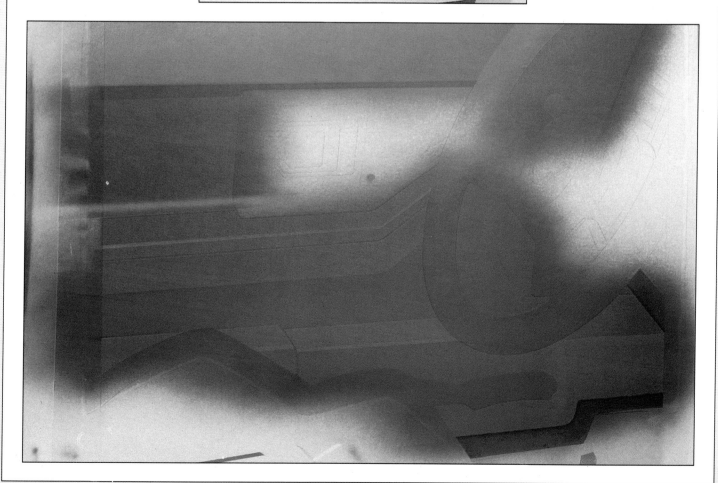

8 *All used masking is again removed. The part to be worked on next is the leather-covered seat. Accordingly, paper is attached to the surrounding area, secured here and there with masking tape, and masking film is placed over the seat itself and masks are cut.*

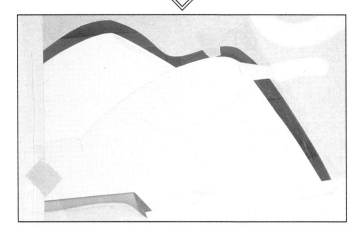

9 *On this surface, the artist wants to ensure that all shadows, seams, creases and so on are rendered as soft as possible to give the impression of the suppleness of the leather. To do this, he first uses loose acetate masks for the shadows between the separate sections of the seat.*

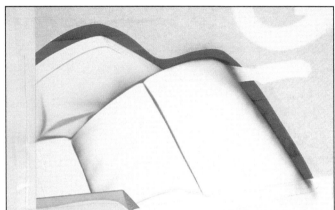

10 *The creases in the leather are rendered freehand, the artist frequently consulting his photographic reference. Loose acetate masks can also be used if slightly harder-looking creases and shadows are required.*

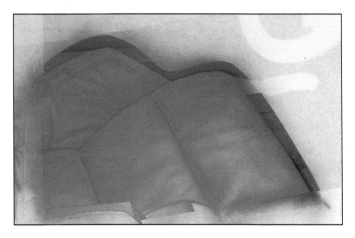

11 *The freehand airbrushing continues. Varying shades of red ink are used to obtain depth and definition. As the artist works, he keeps a check on the balance of tones, and ensures that the texture resembles that of leather — that is, soft and shiny yet slightly grainy.*

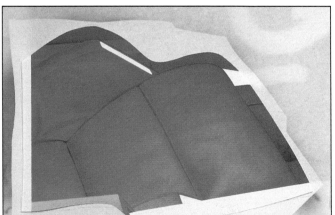

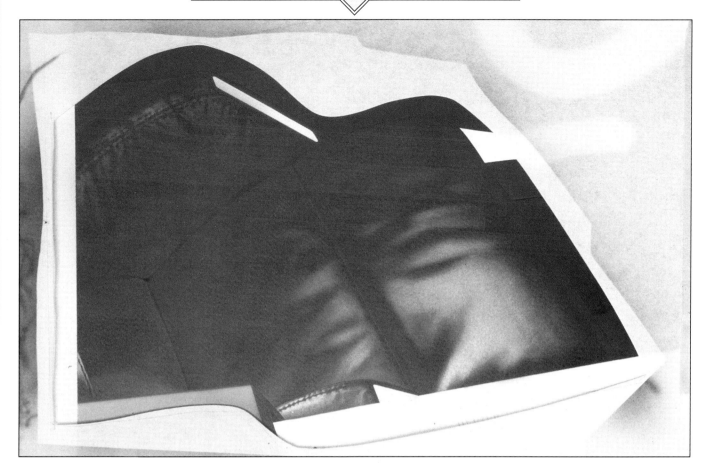

12 The time has come to high-light the creases and seams. The artist lightly sprays some areas with white gouache, using acetate masks to achieve the correct softness. He also scratches back the colour with a scalpel, a technique that is very effective in rendering a leather-like texture.

13 The seat is now finished. All the previous masking is removed, and the image is re-covered as before. This time, masks are cut for all the black and grey areas, except for the steering wheel and gear shift, which will be completed at a later stage.

14 *The artist then sprays these dark areas. He removes the masks a tone at a time – from those parts needing thin black ink up to and including those requiring blue-grey. The matt plastic mirror surround, combining both hard lines and modelled corners, demands special attention.*

15 *A tint of blue is added to all the dark grey and black plastic parts. This is needed because the plastic will eventually reflect the light coming through the transparent tinted windows. All the masking is then removed and any errors in tone or line corrected.*

16 The image is re-covered, and masks are cut out for the side window, the mirror and the sliver of windscreen that can be seen behind the mirror. These are sprayed with a tint of blue, darkest on the windows, which are themselves tinted blue, and lightest on the clear glass of the mirror.

17 The masking is removed, and loose masks are used in the spraying of soft highlights. Harder ones are painted on the edges with a fine brush. The door light is masked and sprayed yellow, darker at the edges and lighter in the centre. The red square under the lock is masked and sprayed.

18 All the masking is removed, revealing the entire image, which is almost complete. All the tones are checked to ensure that they make sense and, if necessary, corrections are made with the air-brush and/or a brush.

19 *Now the steering wheel and the gear shift are covered with masking film, and masks are cut out. Pieces of "instant texture" are placed over both components, rubbed down and the excess cut away. (For a view of the gear shift, see step 22.)*

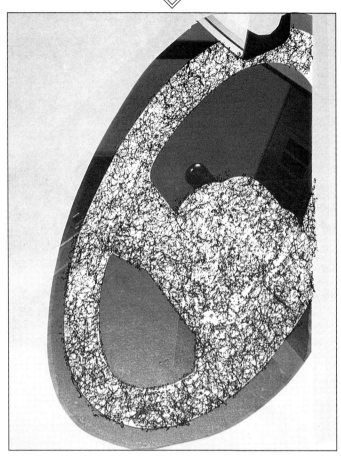

20 *A tint of black ink is sprayed over the "instant texture", the holes in it allowing the ink to reach the artboard. When the ink is dry, the "texture" is lifted off with masking tape. Left behind are two negative images of the "instant texture".*

21 *Black ink is sprayed free-hand on to both the steering wheel and the gear shift. Acetate masks are used on the spokes and centre of the wheel. A subtle reflection of the red of the interior is added to the base of the wheel rim, and a tint of blue is sprayed over the wheel.*

22 *Using white gouache and loose acetate masks, the artist sprays highlights on to the wheel and gear shift. Finer details such as the stitching on the inside rim of the wheel and on the sleeve of the gear shift are achieved both with a brush and by scratching back with a scalpel.*

23 *All masking is removed and replaced. Masks for the badge are cut in the film over the hub of the steering wheel. The artist works from black to the lighter colours, removing the masks one at a time, until the badge is fully painted. Then highlights are added.*

24 *The picture is complete, and the textures and surfaces can be seen in all their variety. Even though most of the components have a matt surface, subtle reflections – the enhanced blue of the sky and the red of the interior – are still present, uniting the interior of the car with the world outside.*

MORE PROFESSIONAL EXAMPLES

▲ The nubbly texture of this Mazda estate car's carpet was created by spraying at low air pressure. Hard masking cut carefully with a scalpel was used to render the crisp outlines of the side panels. The artist, John Harwood, used a ship curve rather than a · French curve to achieve gentle arcs.

▶ This technical illustration of a seat from a Mazda RX7 was also painted by John Harwood. The springs were created with hard masking, finished by the careful hand brushing of reflections and highlights. The arrows were sprayed a uniform, flat blue and then outlined in ink with a technical pen.

TYRES

Although a car's tyres may seem to be the least important part as far as the airbrush artist is concerned, being able to recreate them realistically is vital. It is the tyres that anchor the car to the ground, not only in the real world but also in terms of conveying a car's true solidity and relationship with its surroundings. Unlike the bodywork and trim, for which you will have to rely upon your ability to render the appropriate glistening metallic surface, tyres have a relatively soft, matt surface. The techniques required to reproduce this will differ from those used for metal, the image being much more modelled and diffuse. Brushwork and a steady hand are also needed for the lettering and to indicate the tread (see also *Other Masking Techniques*, p. 37 for tread created with masking fluid). Tyres can also convey movement, and this will be dealt with in a later section.

1 *The tyre is carefully drawn on to tracing paper. Three photographic references are used: one for the basic tyre (from a Corvette); one showing the centre cap clearly; and one showing the range of light and shadow over the whole tyre.*

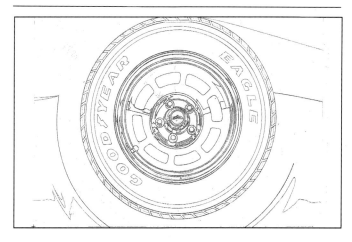

2 *After de-greasing the fine-line artboard with lighter fluid to make the surface absolutely clean, the drawing is transferred using tracing-down paper. Special attention is paid to the different tones of light and dark; these will require separate masks. The lettering will be added later.*

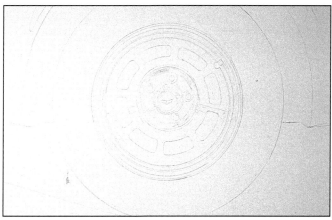

3 *Low-tack self-adhesive film is placed over the trace and all the masks are cut. Care is taken to cut only through the film: if the board is cut, this will leave a mark that cannot be repaired. The first masks to be removed are the areas that will be painted darkest.*

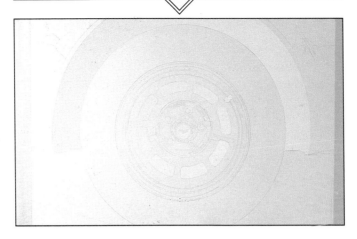

4 *The areas now exposed – under the wheel arch and the slots in the wheel – are then sprayed with black ink. (Lighter colours can later be sprayed over this without altering the dark shade.) These areas of deepest shadow are painted in one overall flat colour.*

5 *The masks covering the next darkest areas are then removed: the tyre itself and the lower half of the bodywork. These are sprayed with black ink. The tyre is modelled – that is, "drawn" with the airbrush so that, by graduating from light to dark, its roundness becomes apparent.*

6 The mask covering the upper half of the bodywork is removed. First, this is sprayed lightly with black, and then with blue. This gives the bodywork a shine with some depth. Next, some more blue is sprayed lightly over the tyre to give a blue-grey tint to the whole car.

7 All the remaining masking film is removed to check progress so far. This is an important step: over-spraying on to masks can make it impossible to get a complete view of a picture, and this can lead to errors and inconsistencies in tonal relationships. All the detail and highlights will be added later.

8 Everything sprayed so far is covered with layout paper; masking film is applied around the edges, leaving the road surface exposed. A mask is then cut from acetate for the shadow to the left of the wheel (the light source is to the right and slightly forward).

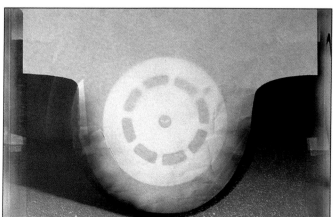

9 First, the road surface is sprayed with black ink, gradually lightening as it emerges from beneath the car. Using a splatter cap, white gouache is sprayed to give the road surface some texture. The shadow of the wheel (formed by the acetate mask) is sprayed. The road is then tinted with blue.

10 *All masks are again removed to check progress. The basic forms have been completed, and the bodywork and tyre have achieved a realistic solidity. The shadow under the tyre has a slightly soft edge because of the loose acetate mask, which allowed air and paint underneath it.*

11 *Using the original drawing and white tracing-down paper, the lettering is carefully traced on to the tyre. This is painted over in white gouache using a brush. The modelling of the tyre is renewed by spraying thin black over the lettering.*

12 *The tyre is completed with the addition of highlights on it and the bodywork. These are applied using both airbrush and paintbrush and acetate masks and masking film. Particular care is taken getting the tyre tread right.*

MORE PROFESSIONAL EXAMPLES

◄ *This Pete Kelly composition of a Mercedes under a tyre may seem quite strange. However, it was actually designed to be a clock face, the 12 spokes of the wheel acting as the "numbers". Because there was no need for realism, the artist simplified the tyre by eliminating the tread.*

▲ This Tyrrell 017 Formula One racing car was created by Mike Hughes with great attention to detail. The tyres have no tread: during races, they heat up and stick to the road surface. The wheels are different colours so that, during pit stops, the appropriate tyres can be replaced quickly.

◀ The simplicity of John Harwood's portrait of a Citroën engine, chassis and tyres (part of which is reproduced here) shows how functional objects can be combined into an aesthetic whole. The tyres were first sprayed with a grey/black tint, and then the tread was rendered with a pen, highlights being added with a brush.

CHROME

It is perhaps the presence of glittering chrome on automobiles that gives them their special appeal to air-brush artists. Grilles, trim, door handles, wing mirrors, bumpers and wheels – all these can be constructed of that flashy-yet-solid metal. This is particularly true of cars of years gone by, and most especially the exuberant American monsters of the 1950s, with their ever-larger tail fins and grinning-toothed grilles. Like every subject in airbrushing, an almost exact facsimile of chrome is achievable as long as you look carefully at what you are going to recreate, take care and time with your initial drawing and choose the correct colours and masks. Here, we will be completing the wheel and tyre begun in the section on tyres. Note the contrast between the relatively soft surface of the tyre and the hard, shiny surface of the wheel.

1 *The initial drawing has been traced down on to the artboard (see Tyres, step 2). Chrome reflections can be confusing, so it may be helpful to shade the darkest areas lightly with a pencil; this will act as a guide when you start spraying.*

2 *Layout paper is used to cover the painting to within 1.25 cm (½ in) of the wheel. This is held in place by the matt low-tack masking film that is, in turn, placed over the wheel. Masks corresponding to the areas to be sprayed darkest in tone are then cut.*

3 *Consulting the photographic reference frequently, the artist first sprays the revealed areas with black ink and then adds blue-grey. Orange is sprayed around the base of the wheel, where the highlight will eventually spill over.*

4 *The paint-obscured masking film is removed and the wheel is checked to ensure that the reflections are building up properly. A new piece of masking film is then placed over the wheel, and masks for the next-darkest areas are cut.*

5 *Grey, blue and orange inks are sprayed over the cut-out areas. It is essential that tones are built up systematically. Chrome comprises shiny, often hard-edged reflections, and so its treatment will be different from the soft, graduated modelling of the tyre.*

6 *The masking film is removed, and a mask is cut to reveal the upper part of the concave wheel, in which all reflections will appear upside down. The reflections of the road and the surrounding land are sprayed. Soft reflections are carried out freehand.*

7 *When so many masks are used, white lines are sometimes left behind. These areas are retouched using both a brush and a loose acetate mask. It is important to carry this out at an early stage, so that tints can be added on top.*

8 *Small, intricate areas such as the wheelnuts are worked, using a brush and the airbrush. Then the whole wheel is covered with film. A mask is cut to reveal the area reflecting the blue sky – at the bottom of the concave wheel. This is sprayed with a mixture of ultramarine and cyan ink.*

9 Using a fine brush, the artist paints further highlights on the edges of the wheel, wheelnuts and cap. Other details are also added by hand. Then, loading the airbrush with white gouache, he sprays over them to give a shine to the chrome.

10 With the paper surround removed, the completed picture of the tyre and wheel is revealed. The contrast between the shiny chrome and the modelled softness of the rubber is obvious, and the car is located in its environment by the different tints and the reflections.

MORE PROFESSIONAL EXAMPLES

◀ This swooping tailfin and sleek chrome bumper, both styles of yesteryear, were rendered by John Spires in ink and gouache. The image is quite stylized, with the chrome bumper reflecting the blue of the car body perhaps more than would be the case in real life.

▶ Robert Corley used mainly inks and acrylics for this dual portrait of a 1924 Mercedes and a Junkers G38 aeroplane. However, the bumper was sprayed lightly with black watercolour, and the extremely fine lines of the grille were achieved by applying black ink and then scratching back with a scalpel.

Difficulty in finding a photograph of a 1959 Corvette forced Vincent Wakerley to adapt one of a 1960 model, using a variety of references showing various 1959 components, particularly a grille and wheelcaps. Finally, all the reflections had to be altered to match each other.

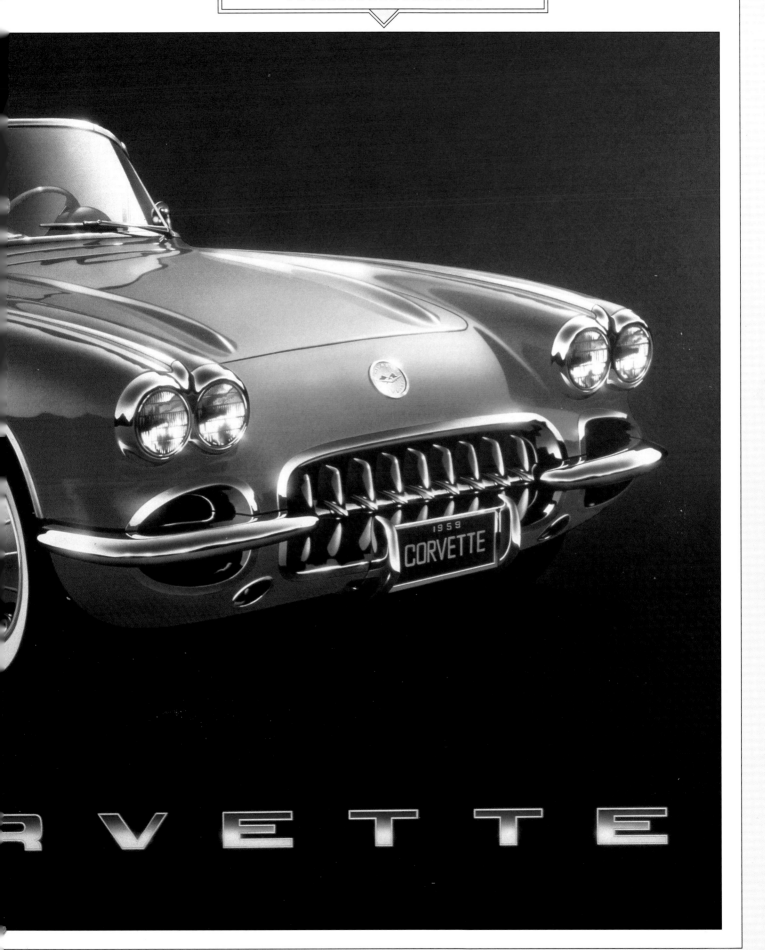

ENGINES

The engine is the heart of an automobile, and rendering an image of one will involve all the technical skills you can muster. The primary aesthetic appeal of machinery is the precision with which the various components are made; if this precision is not matched in your illustration, the effect is lost. One of the techniques for which airbrushing is justly famous is the cutaway view. Most modern engines are hidden beneath metal casings, but this can be easily overcome in an airbrushed portrait simply by removing a portion of the casing to reveal the parts below. The fact that engines are mainly composed of grey metal can pose a daunting problem for artists unaccustomed to painting in monochrome. However, using black-and-white photographs as reference should help, and you can also employ other colours to differentiate between various components.

1 *The engine is carefully drawn and then traced down on to the artboard. (The Corvette lettering and logo on the left will be used for ghosting in the next section.) This type of illustration should always be kept simple.*

2 *The perimeter of the artboard is covered with paper, and masking film is placed over the image. All masks that will be needed are cut, and those covering black areas are removed.*

3 *First, the revealed areas are sprayed black. Then the artist gradually works from dark to blue-grey, removing the relevant masks one by one. Shadows are created both freehand and with the aid of loose acetate masks.*

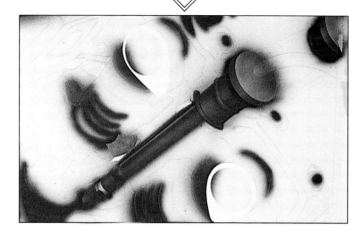

4 *Here, two masks have just been removed, and the revealed parts are awaiting treatment. When rendering surfaces consisting of cast metal, the artist reduces the air pressure in the airbrush to create a speckled effect.*

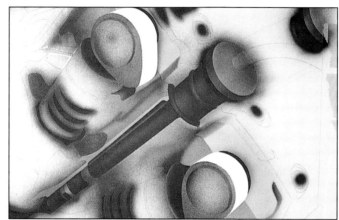

5 *Hard surfaces are given a machine-shine with the addition of subtle reflections rendered freehand. Fine lines are scratched into the valve faces to give a lapped finish. Practice in reflections and highlights will pay off when this type of work is attempted.*

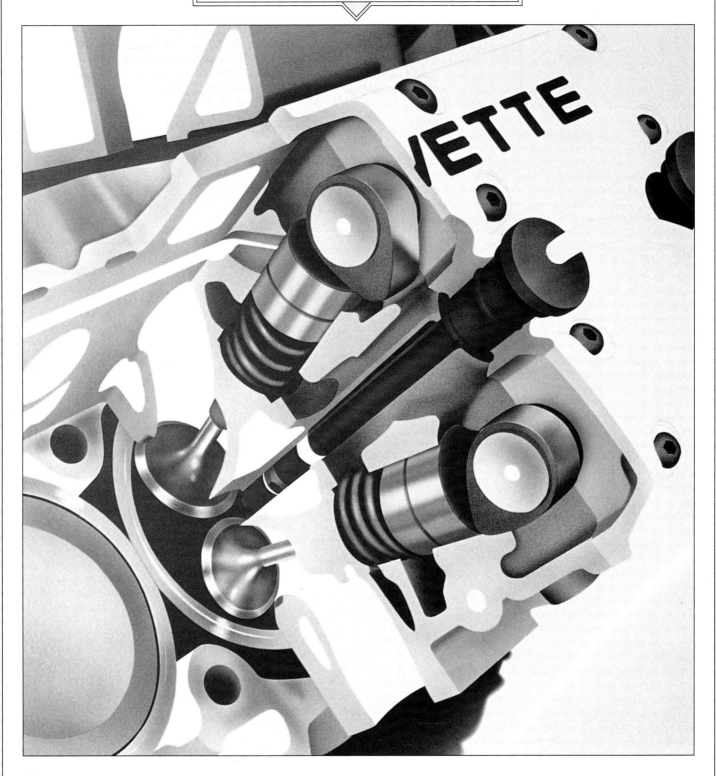

6 *With all the masking removed, this is the story so far. All lines are crisp, and the monochromatic tones add up. Complicated shapes now have a beguiling simplicity, and the way in which the engine works is becoming clearer. The image is covered with new masking film.*

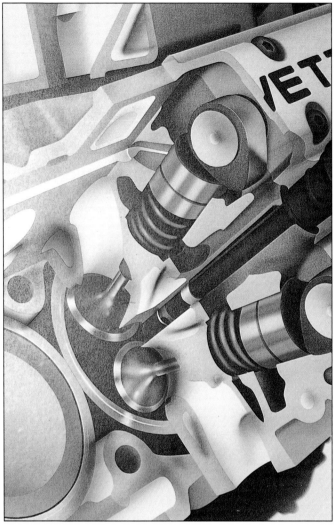

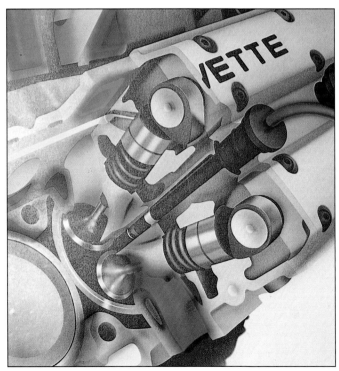

7 Masks are cut for the cam cover, water and oil galleries, induction and exhaust ports and PCV. Now, as the masks are removed, they are carefully placed to one side, ready for re-use. The artist first removes the mask for the cam cover and creates shadows by spraying over a ruler.

8 When the cam cover is completely dry, its mask is replaced, with care taken not to distort the thin plastic. Now work begins on the galleries and ports. Soft light grey shadows are added freehand and through acetate masks to give a three-dimensional feel to the cylinder head.

9 Colours are added so that the various components can be distinguished: yellow for oil, light blue for induction, red for exhaust, green for water and orange for PCV breathers. The artist works from the darkest colours to the lightest, replacing masks as he goes.

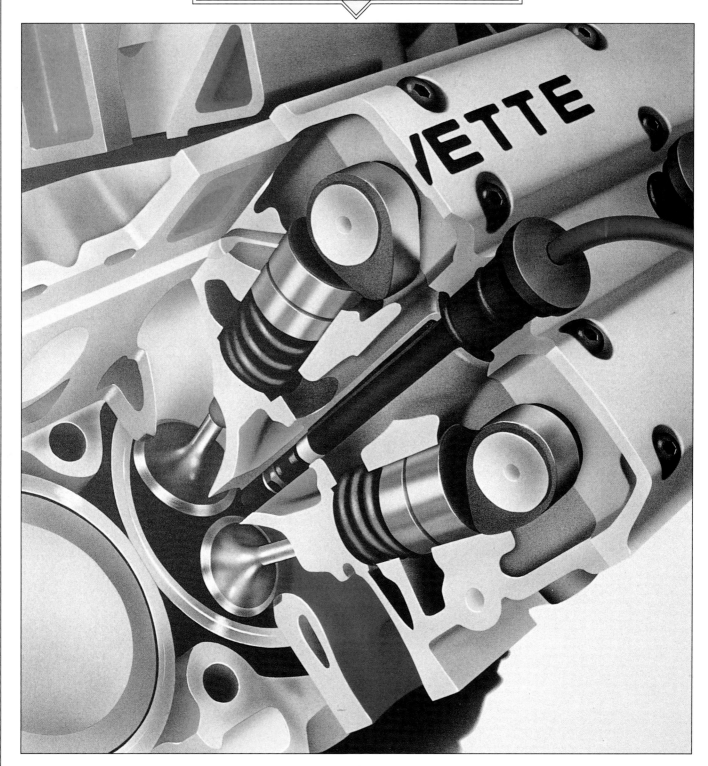

10 All the masking is removed, and the picture is checked. Finally, highlights are added with a fine brush and by scraping back with a scalpel. However, these should not be overdone: the object of this type of illustration is to be informative, not artistic.

GHOSTING

The previous sequence showed the rendering of a cutaway of an engine. However, it is also possible to indicate the interior *and* exterior view of an engine, simultaneously, by means of a technique called *ghosting*. Even more than the cutaway, this is probably the technique to which the airbrush is best suited, with its ability to spray very thin layers of paint or ink to create an uncanny dual illusion of solidity and transparency. Ghosting can be carried out in two ways. The exterior of the central object can be rendered uniformly solid, and then the inner contents indicated by being lightly drawn up over the image of the outer surface. Or, the inner contents can be fully described, with the outer surface lightly sprayed on top, as in the following sequence, with the added problem of ghosting a logo that is moulded into the metal surface.

1 *The Corvette logo and lettering have already been drawn up (see Engines, step 1). The artist covers the image of the engine with matt masking film. He then traces down the logo and lettering directly on to this, using coloured tracing-down paper so the drawing will be visible.*

2 *Masks are cut and removed. The artist begins by spraying the lettering with a black tint, using very light pressure to preserve the essential transparency. The logo will be visible only by its shadow, so the edges are sprayed with grey ink, and then only a very light tint is applied to the rest.*

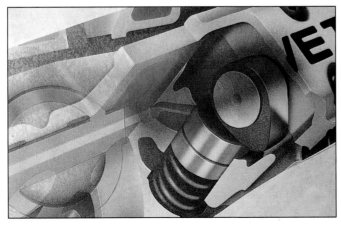

3 *All the masking is removed and the image is examined for balance and for any errors that may have crept in. Using a fine brush, the artist touches in various details and covers a few white lines that have occurred where masks have overlapped.*

4 *The cam cover is remasked, masks are cut for the bolts securing the cam cover and these are lightly sprayed in dark grey-black. Finally, all the masking is removed, and the "ghost" of the shadow of the upper cam cover is lightly sprayed over the engine. The artist sprays across a ruler to achieve a clean, sharp edge.*

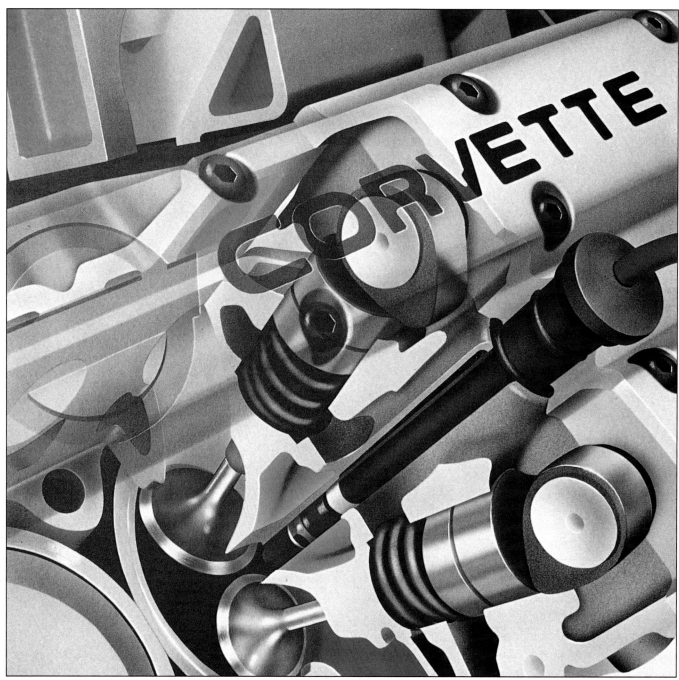

MORE PROFESSIONAL EXAMPLES

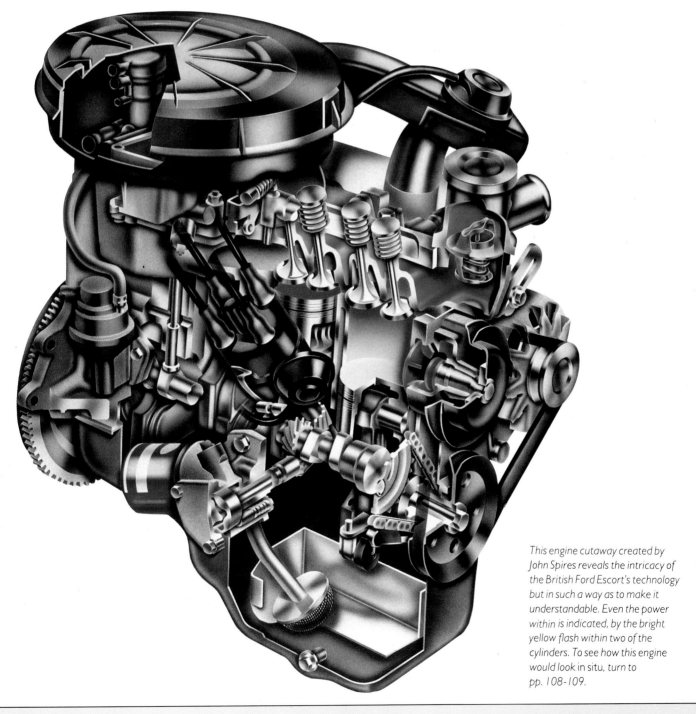

This engine cutaway created by John Spires reveals the intricacy of the British Ford Escort's technology but in such a way as to make it understandable. Even the power within is indicated, by the bright yellow flash within two of the cylinders. To see how this engine would look in situ, turn to pp. 108-109.

This masterpiece of the cutaway by John Spires comprises almost every aspect of the Ford Escort, including the construction of a seat and the springs and brakes of the front wheel. Very little ghosting has been done; all there is, is contained within the wing area. Instead, the artist has judiciously deleted inconsequential parts to reveal what happens where and why.

▲ This group portrait of a Toyota cylinder and cars was achieved by Richard Duckett using gouache and acrylic paint, with precise masking and brushwork. The cars – a Lamborghini Countach, Peugeot 205 GTi, Porsche 911 and Honda Civic – give an added dimension to a technical illustration.

▶ With these cylinders and pistons, John Harwood has made a visual statement about the efficiency of combustion of two different brands of petrol. Because the combustion was the focus, the engine parts were stylized; instead of comprising matt metal, they were rendered in chrome.

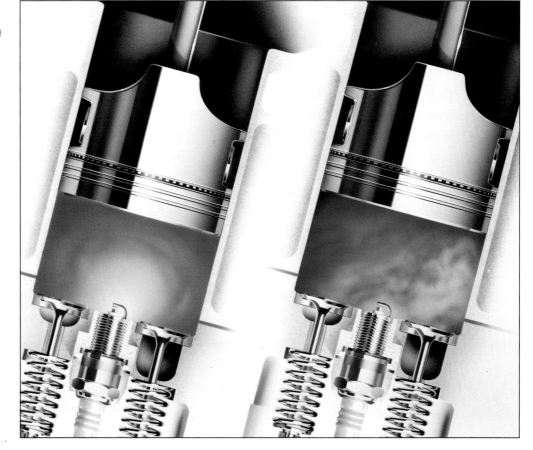

This Isuzu Piazza turbo engine was given an exaggerated perspective by Richard Duckett to lend the image added dynamism. While most of the rendering was straightforward, the intercooler at the front incorporates ghosting to explain how it works – the point of this illustration.

▼ To create this skeleton of a Bedford van prototype, John Harwood had to work from engineer's drawings. All the tyre treads and much of the details of the engine were carried out with a pen. Attention was paid to tonal values to create a unified whole that maintains constant interest.

MOVEMENT – WHEELS

Although automobiles can be appreciated in all their static glory – the flowing lines, the crisp reflections, the precise detailing – it is as a moving machine that the car has achieved its special place in the hearts of millions. It has become almost a cliché to render movement by means of off-white streaks spinning off the various parts of a car, as if hastily puffed clouds of smoke are mysteriously emanating from its metal bodywork. While this may be quite suitable for a comic strip, the true professional will see that an illusion of movement can be created far more subtly, by the sparing use of blurring in the moving parts and, especially, the tyres and wheels. Also not to be forgotten when creating an impression of speed is the road surface, which, with only the simplest of treatments, can be made to seem part of the speeding imagery.

1 *The image of this Formula One racing car and driver was drawn on to tracing paper and then traced down on to the artboard. All the lettering and other precision work has been carefully executed, and an indication has been given of the deepest shadows underneath.*

2 *The artboard is covered with a sheet of paper. A square is cut into this, to within 1.25 cm (½ in) of the actual illustration; the edges of the square are secured with masking tape. Low-tack masking film is then placed over the car and driver, and masks are cut.*

3 *Using blue ink, the sky is sprayed. The height of the air-brush is varied to give a slight illusion of depth. Then, with a paint brush and grey ink, long streaks are painted along the road surface, to give a subtle impression of movement.*

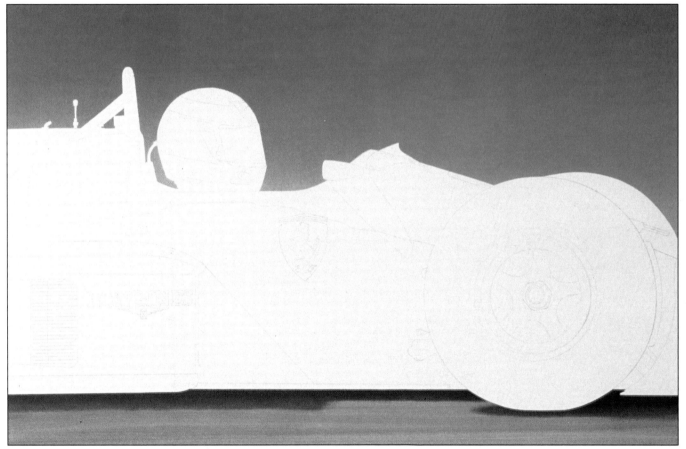

4 *The road surface is given just a tint of blue to match the sky. Black ink is then sprayed over a previously cut, loose acetate mask to render the deepest shadows under the car. Care is taken to indicate the two wheels at the front of the car. The masking tape and masks are then removed.*

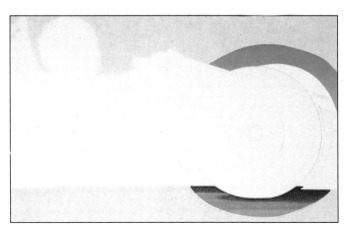

5 *Everything but the wheel and tyres is covered with a paper mask; those parts left bare are covered with masking film. Using a scalpel, the artist cuts along all the lines showing through the film. The film covering the darkest areas – the tyres, wheel slots and wheelnut – is removed.*

6 *The dark areas are sprayed with black ink. The artist uses loose masks for the curves on the tyre and for the wheel slots. This technique gives a soft edge, with the result that the wheel and tyre appear to be moving.*

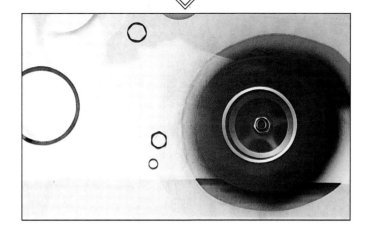

7 *All the masks on the tyres and wheel are removed. Then the whole area – the dark parts as well as the metal wheel – are tinted carefully with sky blue ink. This is important if all parts of the car are to appear to be within the environment of the picture.*

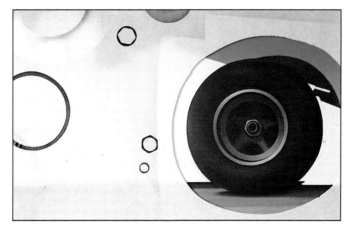

8 *Using loose masks, the artist adds highlights to the tyre and metal wheel. For small details, such as the wheelnut, a fine paintbrush is employed. Alternatively, the colour could be gently scratched back with a scalpel.*

9 *Loading his brush with thin white gouache, the artist sprays a few light streaks on to the tyre in the direction of its movement, again using a loose mask for a soft effect. The streaks are further indications of motion – effective without being crude.*

10 *A loose mask is cut to give a rough suggestion of the lettering on the tyre. Spraying with thin white gouache, the artist again moves the mask in the same direction as the tyre in motion, thus blurring the letters. White highlights are then sprayed on to the wheel.*

MOVEMENT – CAR BODY

As was seen in the previous sequence, a car's movement can be implied by the subtle use of blurring and streaks on the vehicle's various parts. When you arrive at the car body itself, however, other things must be taken into consideration. In real life, as a car passes, it will all appear blurred, but there isn't much point in reproducing this if what you are interested in is the car itself. Therefore, you should think of your car portrait as the equivalent of a photograph shot with a very fast lens: the camera has clicked at the same speed as the carbody is travelling, with the result that, for the most part, it appears static with all its detailing clearly visible, while the tyres and wheels, which are moving faster than the car body, appear blurred. All that is required to imply movement in the car body are just a few sparing touches.

1 *The artboard is covered with paper, which is then cut to reveal the area to be sprayed. This is covered with masking film, and masks are cut. The masks for the shadows are removed, and, using dark red ink, the artist sprays graduated tones, darkest near the car parts casting the shadows.*

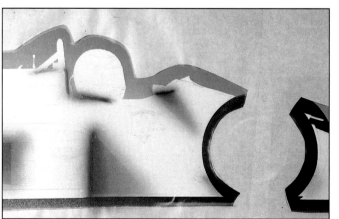

2 *All the body masks are removed, except those covering details. Using loose acetate masks, the artist sprays the reflection along the side of the car body, blurring it slightly towards the back of the car. This is done by lifting the mask and allowing spray to get underneath it.*

3 *A bright red ink is sprayed over the car body. The areas that are to be highlighted are sprayed a slightly lighter red. Here, the artist is creating different shades of red by building up layers of tints. The red on the side of the driver's helmet is also sprayed.*

4 *A light tint of blue is sprayed on to the top of the car, to imply the reflection of the blue sky in the shiny fibre-glass surface. Like the blue tint on the tyre, wheel and road surface, this is necessary to place the car within its environment.*

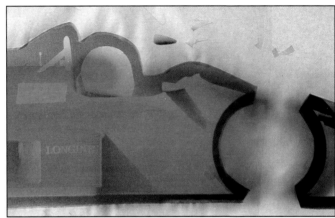

5 *The remaining masks are removed, and the whole car body is covered with a new sheet of masking film. Masks of the dark grey and black areas are then carefully cut. Small details and white lettering will be added later.*

6 *The artist begins spraying the black areas – including the black lettering and the shadow in front of the wheels – and then gradually works towards grey. A highlight is carefully incorporated on the roll bar, to give the impression of roundness.*

7 *The film covering the lighter shadow areas is removed, and these are sprayed grey. The radiator is first sprayed a dark grey, and then thin, light grey lines are hand-painted with a fine brush, using a ruler as a guide. Finally, the radiator's shadow is added, using a loose acetate mask.*

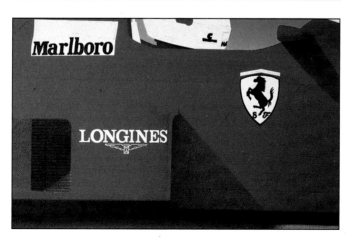

8 *All the remaining masking film is removed. The small details and lettering on the car body and helmet are then hand-painted in their appropriate colours, using a fine brush. The stickers and badges, both those on the side of the car and the parts that are just visible on the bonnet, are treated in the same way.*

9 *The illustration is covered with paper. This is cut to reveal the driver's helmet, which, in turn, is covered with masking film. Then masks are cut for the areas that are to be sprayed the darkest.*

10 *The very darkest areas – the reflective screen, the wire connecting the microphone in the helmet to the radio, and the helmet trim and shadow at the neck – are sprayed a dark blue/black.*

11 *The masks covering the colour areas on the top and bottom of the helmet are then removed. These areas are sprayed blue – darker at the neck and lighter towards the top. An acetate mask is used for the dimple in the side of the helmet.*

12 *The remaining mask on the driver's helmet is removed. A graduated blue/grey shadow is sprayed on to this area to make the helmet screen appear rounded. Highlights and other details will be added later.*

13 *All the masks are now removed. The image is covered with paper, which is cut to reveal the stickers and badges. These are covered with masking film, and masks are cut for the different colour areas. These are removed, and spraying is carried out in the following order: green, red, yellow.*

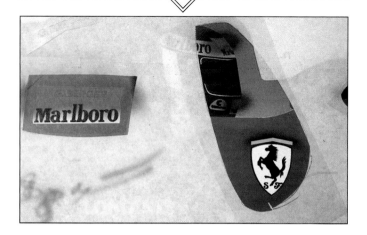

14 *With the masks and paper removed, highlights of white gouache are sprayed through acetate masks as they are moved in the direction of the car's movement, to soften and blur them and give the impression of speed. The finer highlights, such as those on the helmet screen, are painted by hand.*

15 *To give an even stronger impression of movement, lettering and details (especially on the roll bar) are blurred by lightly spraying both white gouache and black ink over loose acetate masks.*

16 *In this close-up of the left-hand side of the finished picture, the blurred portions can be seen clearly. The helmeted driver, on the other hand, is in sharp focus – just as he, as the centre of attention, should be.*

17 *This detail of the right-hand side of the completed image reveals the final relationship between the car body and the moving wheel and tyre. On its own, the body appears static and almost one-dimensional. With the addition of the tyre, however, the image is one of speed.*

MORE PROFESSIONAL EXAMPLES

▲ *Almost everything in this Pete Beazis composition is moving: the vehicles in the centre as well as the tyre (seeming to travel both around and forward) that acts as a frame for the action. The static lettering simply accentuates the movement of the other parts.*

▶ *This stunning example of a Peugeot 405 in motion was created by John Harwood. The original reference was of a red car so the artist had to alter all the paintwork as well as incorporating new reflections. The image was rendered primarily in acrylics, with the smashed fence drawn in black ink with a technical pen.*

The movement of this Honda
Williams racing car by John
Harwood has been stylized, with
the road surface rendered in grey
stripes and the "whoosh lines"
equally unrealistic but effective.
The tyre blurring was achieved by
anchoring an acetate mask with a
compass point and spraying round
it little by little.

At first glance, this Vincent Wakerley racing car may seem to be static. However, on a closer look, it can be seen that the depth holes in the treadless tyres have been streaked, and that the road surface is blurred. These hints of motion are contrasted by the super-sharp lettering.

REFLECTIONS

So far, we have dealt individually with chrome, paint-work, windscreens and lights. Now we put together all the techniques that have been investigated with these into a final sequence. This fine example of the chrome-encrusted monsters that once cruised the high-ways and byways of America in the 1950s demonstrates more than any other type of car exactly how important is a deft and sure hand in the rendering of reflections, and how vital it is to be aware of the relationship between the subject and its surroundings. Here the automobile itself, with its unashamedly excessive chrome decoration and the upward tilt of its tailfin, is a solid reflection of the optimism and the enthusiasm for material things that characterized the post-war era. And the reflections in the chrome, glass and paintwork — of a city skyline and blue sky — echo the mood.

1 *The image is drawn carefully on to tracing paper, and then it is traced down on to the artboard. The image is covered with paper, and the chrome areas are cut out and covered with masking film. Masks are then cut for all the reflections in and shadows on the chrome.*

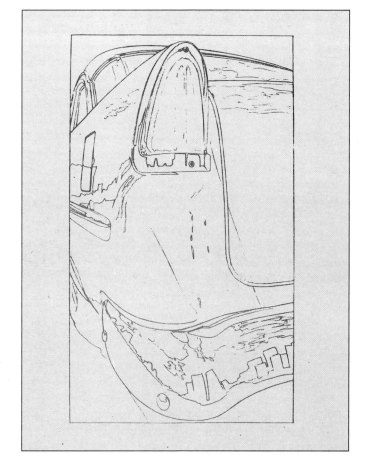

2 *The artist first deals with the black areas on the window surround, tail light surround, side chrome detailing and bumper. The skyline will eventually be shown in high relief. The tyre, the deep shadow beneath the car and the road surface are also sprayed in.*

3 *The masks covering the next-darkest areas are removed, and the revealed parts (including the back window) are sprayed with a dark blue-grey. The masks on the upper part of the car are removed to check the range of tones. The tiny crossheaded masks of the light screws can be seen.*

4 *Coloured reflections in the bumper are then inserted. An image of the brown road surface is added to the bottom of the bumper, and the distorted dark-red reflections of the tail light and the boot are added to the top.*

5 *The parts of the car that clearly reflect the sky are now dealt with. They are first masked and cut, and then sprayed lightly with a mixture of ultramarine and cyan ink. Red is then painted on the side window surround and on the right side of the tail light surround.*

6 *All the masking is removed, and highlights are added using white gouache. These are done freehand, with both airbrush and fine sable brush, and with the use of a loose acetate mask. Special attention is paid to the curve of the back window, the bolts and screws and the hint of the wheel.*

7 *In this detail of the rear bumper, the reflections of the ground and the silhouetted cityscape can clearly be seen. Modelling has been done on the reflections of both the blue sky and the red boot and tail light. A narrow band of highlight has been added all along the bottom of the bumper.*

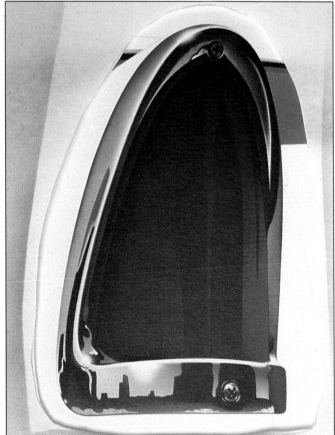

8 *The entire image is covered with paper, and the area of the tail light is cut out. This is covered with masking film, and a mask of the lens is cut out. The shadow and reflection in the revealed area are first sprayed a dark red, and then an overall tint of a medium red is applied.*

9 *A faint white reflection consisting of thin white gouache is sprayed over the lens. Then the artist sprays a harder, stronger reflection on to the far right-hand side of the lens, using masking film to do so.*

10 *All the masking is removed, and fine black lines denoting the boot and the fuel tank door are painted with a finely pointed sable brush. The image is covered with masking film to reveal the bodywork. Masks are cut, and those for the darkest areas are removed. These are sprayed dark red.*

11 *Further reflections are added, primarily with the use of acetate masks to guarantee a softened precision. However, some of the more jagged reflections, such as those on the side and under the tail light, are created freehand.*

12 *The artist then sprays a tint of red over all of the bodywork. He is careful to graduate the tone so that the bodywork is lighter towards the tops of the curves of the wing, roof and boot, which reflect light from the sky.*

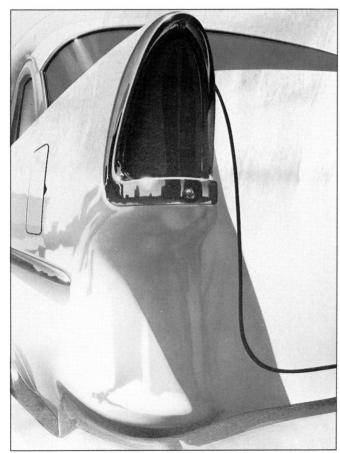

13 *A hint of blue sky reflection is sprayed on the tops of the roof, wing and boot. Highlights on the bodywork are then added using gouache and, in some cases, masking film to give sharp edges.*

MORE PROFESSIONAL EXAMPLES

▶ *This car, and its reflections, are all pure fantasy, created for the book* Lots of Kisses. *Nigel Tidman combined a number of references to come up with this unique vehicle.*

◀ *Mystery surrounds the upside-down reflection of a car in the bonnet of this Robert Corley creation. The primary composition is very simple, with only a minimum of detail rendered.*

The reflections in the paintwork of this classic car, a Jaguar D-type (hence the feline lounging above it), were rendered by Nick Farmer in a slightly opaque watercolour, using both hand brushing and airbrushing. Much of the detail in the reflections was "drawn" by being sprayed close up.

Hard metallic reflections are contrasted by Vincent Wakerley with graded skin tones. Automobile and girl's body interact: the car's crisp highlights are echoed in the highlighted area on one side of the girl, and the swimsuit cut-outs are repeated in the car's fluted bodywork.

The subtlety of gradation achieved by Keith Harmer for the paintwork of this Porsche Turbo was made easier by the use of an airbrush with an extra-fine nozzle. There are two light sources: one is to the right, and the other, responsible for the deep shadows, is the sunset.

INDEX

CREDITS

CREDITS

Every effort has been made to obtain copyright clearance for the illustrations in this book and we do apologize if any omissions have been made.

Quarto would like to thank the following for their help with this publication.

p 2 Vincent Wakerley, Visage Design. **p 7** courtesy of Smithsonian Institute. **p 9** *top*: courtesy of Robert Opie; *bottom*: courtesy of Smithsonian Institute. **p 10** Joe Lawrence. **pp 13-15** photography: Paul Forrester. **pp 16-17** photography: Colin Barker. **pp 18-19** photography: Paul Forrester. **p 21** *left*: Gavin Macleod, courtesy of Meiklejohn Illustration; *right*: Pete Kelly, courtesy of Meiklejohn Illustration. **p 23** photography: Colin Barker. **p 24** Vincent Wakerley, Visage Design. **p 25** *top*: John Spires, courtesy of Artists Inc; *bottom*: Robin Koni, courtesy of Meiklejohn Illustration. **p 28** photography: Paul Forrester. **pp 29-33** Brian Robson, Visage Design. **pp 34-36** photography: Paul Forrester.

p 37 Brian Robson, Visage Design. **pp 38-45** Vincent Wakerley, Visage Design. **p 46** *top*: Pete Kelly, courtesy of Meiklejohn Illustration; *below*: John Harwood. **p 47** John Harwood. **pp 48-49** Vincent Wakerley, Visage Design. **p50** *top*: Keith Harmer, courtesy of Blue Chip Illustration; *below*: John Harwood. **p 51** *top*: John Harwood; *below*: Pete Kelly, courtesy of Meiklejohn Illustration. **pp 52-53** John Harwood. **p54** Pete Kelly, courtesy of Meiklejohn Illustration. **p 55** *top*: Robert Corley, courtesy of Aart; *below*: Gavin Macleod, courtesy of Meiklejohn Illustration. **pp 56-65** Vincent Wakerley, Visage Design. **p 66** *top*: Pete Kelly, courtesy of Meiklejohn Illustration; *below*: Keith Harmer, courtesy of Blue Chip Illustration. **p 67** Gavin Macleod, courtesy of Meiklejohn Illustration. **pp 68-69** Pete Kelly, courtesy of Meiklejohn Illustration. **PP 70-71** John Harwood. **p 72** Gavin Macleod, courtesy of Meiklejohn Illustration. **p 73** John Spires, courtesy of

Artists Inc. **pp 74-83** Vincent Wakerley, Visage Design. **pp 84-85** John Harwood. **pp 86-89** Vincent Wakerley, Visage Design. **p 90** Pete Kelly, courtesy of Meiklejohn Illustration. **p 91** *top*: Mike Hughes; *bottom*: John Harwood. **pp 92-95** Vincent Wakerley, Visage Design. **p96** John Spires, courtesy of Artists Inc. **p 97** Robert Corley, courtesy of Aart. **pp 98-106** Vincent Wakerley, Visage Design. **pp 107-109** John Spires, courtesy of Artists inc. **p 110** *top*: Richard Duckett, courtesy of Aircraft; *below*: John Harwood. **p 111** *top*: Richard Duckett, courtesy of Aircraft; *below*: John Harwood. **pp 112-121** Vincent Wakerley, Visage Design. **p 122** Pete Beazis, courtesy of Aart. **pp 123-125** John Harwood. **pp 126-133** Vincent Wakerley, Visage Design. **p 134** Robert Corley, courtesy of Aart. **p 135** Nigel Tidman, courtesy of Meiklejohn Illustration. **pp 136-137** Nick Farmer. **pp 138-139** Vincent Wakerley, Visage Design. **pp 140-141** Keith Harmer, courtesy of Blue Chip Illustration.